THE WORLD AS POWER

THE WORLD AS POWER

POWER AS LIFE

BY

JOHN WOODROFFE

GYAN

Published by

Gyan Publishing House
5, Ansari Road
Daryaganj, New Delhi-110002
Phone: 011-47034999, 9811692060
E-mail: books@gyanbooks.com

Distribution Network
gyanbooks.com
India, USA, Canada, UK, Australia

ISBN: 978-93-6280-015-2 (PB)
First Published, 1922

2nd Impression 2024

Printed at: Gyan Press, Delhi.

THE WORLD AS POWER
Author: JOHN WOODROFFE

THE WORLD AS POWER

POWER AS LIFE

THE WORLD AS POWER

POWER AS LIFE

BY

SIR JOHN WOODROFFE

PUBLISHERS:

GANESH & Co., MADRAS

1922

FOREWORD

I TAKE the opportunity given by the publication of the second volume of this series to deal with a criticism on the first which affects all. I am therein described as an "adherent" of "Shaktaism" and as "commending" the acceptance of such doctrine to others. It is true that I think that this doctrine has been misunderstood and has been the subject (on the whole) of unjust judgments. I think also that it is, in its highest presentment, a grand and inspiring system (by which I do not mean that it is the only one, or that it is without defect); otherwise probably I should not have concerned myself with it. I desire however to say here that I do not write as an "adherent" of this, or any other philosophical system or religious sect whatever, but as a free-thinker and free-companion: "Neither Burgundian nor Armagnac." *Nullius addictus jurare in verba magistri.* But, as I have said elsewhere in describing *Shākta* teaching and

Vedānta I write from that standpoint. Nor do I, *pace* my critic, make light of, and still less deny, the utility of Reason or its efficacy to give us the truth within the system of which it is a part. But the Truth as it lies beyond that system is directly realised as it is in Itself, that is beyond Mind not by Reason but by a Full Experience (*Samādhi*) which is not a "sleep" except to the gross world and is an awakening in the supersensible world. Those who talk in this fashion show want of knowledge of their own Scripture. There the highest praise is bestowed on reason. See for instance the Chapter on *Vichāra* in the Yoga-Vāshishtha. Moreover Vedānta does not accept the intuitionalism which discards intellect. On the contrary the Brihadāranyaka Upanishad says that the Self must be thought upon and deeply pondered (*Mantavyo, Nidhidhyāsitavyah*). What else is the meaning of *Jnāna-Yoga!*

Nor, notwithstanding my personal views of the Scripture, do I "commend" it to anyone. What others choose to believe is their affair in which I have no desire to interfere unasked. One of the many notions, for which we are indebted to the profound thought of India, is the fundamental doctrine of Competency or *Adhikāra* which I hope to make the subject of one of this series of volumes. That Doctrine involves this—that there is a mental as well as physical food—a mental as well as physical stomach and digestion.

Talking of food it is curious to note here (see Professeur Picard "La Science Moderne" 245) that all the characteristics of living Matter such as its equilibrium, chemical and anatomic organisation are now regarded by the great majority of Biologists as secondary qualities in comparison with nutrition which is considered by them to be the essential attribute of Life. It is noteworthy that in this ancient Indian doctrine also, emphasis is laid on the physiology of Nutrition, all the main *Vāyus* except *Udāna* being concerned with this function of "living" substance.

Indirectly and on the whole, man tends to the Truth, but directly and immediately what he holds to or seeks is not the truth, but the truth which he *wants*. It is the cravings of his psychical being which he satisfies. This is the meaning of the phrase " will to believe ". If there be a really detached search for truth it is excessively rare. He is a foolish and inconsiderate man who would deprive others of the meal of food, material or intellectual, which satisfies them, though it may not please him. A celebrated German Theosophist was I believe commonly wont to commence his addresses with the observation " I am now going to tell you a story ". Well I also am telling a story. It interests me but I am the last person to persuade others to accept it if they be themselves indifferent or unwilling. I am not seeking " converts " nor trying to " prove " that any one is " wrong ". If, in answering an internal urge to write, I can please others besides myself so much the better. My account of the main Indian Concepts may be of use either to those who are disposed to think the same way, or to those who simply want to know the facts. If the books are of use to any one in either way that is enough for me. Should anyone think that they are of no use, that also is enough; for I will not dispute the point with him. If his own theories held in good faith really satisfy him, I will certainly not "commend" to him any other. Each will answer the speculative questions which all ask, particularly to-day, according to their general theoretic views, the product of their intellectual make-up and temperament. As regards this, all that is required is sincerity, good faith and that openness of mind which is necessary for a progressive self-development.

But all can with confidence become adherents of the Religion of Health, procuring it for themselves and others and relieving their sufferings. Health = Hale = Whole or *Pūrna*. To be *whole* physically, psychically, and spiritually is to be *well*. The contrary of wholeness (*Apūrna*) is Disease. And so it is said *Apūrnam-manyatā Vyādhi*—"the sense of imperfection, that is want of wholeness, is Disease". In, with, or as the Whole, man has life here and hereafter. So one of the *Chakras* in the great *Shrīyantra* is called *Sarvarogahara* or the Destroyer of all Disease which is *Adharma*. Shiva is called *Mrityunjaya* or "Conqueror of Death". As such above his head is shown the Moon shedding streams of Nectar (*Amrita* = Deathlessness) over His upright body. After all it is what a man *is* and *does* which counts. The notion that mere cleverness is enough is not a Hindu one. What is the use of talking of the *Ātmā* and so on if one has helped no one. And so in the Shākta Scriptures, as in others, emphasis is laid on *Kriyā* (action) which however may be given a more extended sense than that in which it is there ordinarily used.

To pass to the subject matter of this book I personally (like indeed, I suppose, most people) do not believe that Life is merely as Claude Bernard said a "fermentation," or that a true theory of it can be based on the now (with some) fashionable "colloidal solution". It has been said that, for the majority of Biologists, vital phenomena are merely physico-chemical phenomena. Nevertheless the Vitalist School is on a truer track. If I remember rightly it was an English Chemist who lately observed that the more Matter is studied the clearer it is seen, that it is *away* from Matter (as such) and in the opposite direction that the solution, if any, of Life will be found. As regards the subject of this Volume I believe in the "simplist" solution that Life, as we know it, is a power (as the Life of all lives) of the Supreme Power (*Parāshakti*). J. H. Fabre, the celebrated Naturalist and incomparable observer (as Darwin called him)—said: "I can't say I *believe* in God. I *see* Him. Without Him I understand nothing: without Him all is darkness." The question is not so much the existence of God but what sort of God. Philosophers and scientists would less grudgingly give to this Power the name of "God" were it not for the crude, ridiculous and even hateful notions which the beliefs of some have associated with this word. Merely physical explanations have availed nothing and will avail nothing. The Vedānta has dealt with the question very profoundly in distinguishing the Vital Body (*Prānamaya Kosha*) from the Physical Body (*Annamaya Kosha*) and in making the lower Mind-Body (*Manomaya Kosha*) which is the vehicle of all the animal instincts, the essence of the former. Life and instinct are wondrous things the sight of which evoke the sentiment of worship. Neither results from Matter. The explanation must be sought not below but above it in the Supreme Intelligence which they emphatically proclaim. J. H. Fabre conceived the relation between instinct and organ as analogous to that between Soul and Body. Instinct is an incorporeal element characterised by a native, infallible and irresistible impulse, superior to the organism as well as to sensibility, though it is not separate from, or completely independent, of these.

As regards evolution also, it would I think say that the separate creation of species is a truer notion than the theory that a higher species evolves from a lower one. For each species is a form of Divine Power (*Daivi Shakti*). If for example A, B, C, be three distinct species in an ascending scale from A to C, it is not A which produces B, nor B which produces C, but it is the one Power (*Mahāshakti*) which produces A, B and C. That Power which has appeared as A, appears also as B, and will next appear as C. B as an ascending type does not owe its ascent to A the lower type, but is a fresh pulsing-forth (*Prasara*) of Power, with a view to liberate Consciousness which appeared as A, now appears as B, and will appear as C. Some Christian writers claim to be "liberal" in repudiating what they call the "crude" view according to which the Creator is perpetually "interfering" with His work. But in my opinion it is more true to say that every act of creation, maintenance, and dissolution in past, present or future is directly His. In the same way it is futile to search for the "missing link" as a lost *form* intermediate between A and B and B and C. The real link is the Supreme Power which produces each. So in a tree, one main branch does not derive from another but from a trunk common to both. This view is not based on any disrespect for Matter, which is as much a form of the Supreme Power in this doctrine as is Life or Mind. As Professor P. N. Mukhyopâdhyâya so well says in his Note appended to this volume—"to those who see the All (*Pūrna*) there is no difference, except formal, when Life is materialised or when Matter is vitalised, or when Spirit is materialised or again when everything is spiritualised". If there has been any People who, taking them all in all, have seen things as they are and seen them "whole" it is the Hindus.

It is not enough to dispose of a solution to say that it is "materialistic". The difficulty in the way of the acceptance of such a solution arises from the nature of Matter itself. If we say, as Professor Tyndall did, that Matter contains the potency of all Life, we are using the word "Matter" in a sense which is not the ordinary one and trying to say something which is stated much better in this Indian Scripture, according to which Matter *as such*, that is as the *crust* or end of the *involving* process is not as such potent to produce Life which is part of the *evolving* process. It is the Power, of which Matter is a gross manifestation, which is able to organise Matter into "living" form, which is the first stage on the way towards liberation from Matter and thus towards Pure Experience. One of the chief keys to an understanding of Indian Philosophy is to remember that all its schemes *begin with everything*. Creation, evolution or whatever else it be called, is only the appearance in subtle and gross forms of an inherent tendency in pure Being—Consciousness, as the *nidus* of all the manifested tendencies or *Sangskāras*. One cannot get out of a bag more than has been put into it. If it is not put there in the beginning, it will not be got out in the end. Thus Life manifests in form. Life has no origin except as manifesting in a particular form. But Life has, in itself, no origin, for it is but a limited aspect of Eternal Being in all Its fullness. Consciousness again has not itself *evolved*. It is gradually *liberated* which is quite a different notion. It is not a product of Matter. If it be not assumed in the beginning it will not be found at the end. It is eternal. Its existence is as a contraction (*Sangkocha*) through association with Mind and Matter. And so with these last two. As constituting shapes they appear and pass away. But in the form of a potency to appear as such--a potency in the Cosmic Will—they had never, according to Vedānta, a beginning as they will never have an end.

The practical effect of a philosophy or religion is of primary importance. In this case the aim is Wholeness and Power and that is the effect of practical working or *Sādhanā* as distinct from mere theorising. The high *Sādhanā* (for there are several degrees) is self-purification and the worship of God as *Shaktimān* or the Supreme Possessor of Power. I hope to deal with *Sādhanā* in a future volume. *Shakti* means "Power" and a *Shākta* is a worshipper of it in Its Supreme form. Then following this, entry is made upon the highest stage which is *Jnāna-yoga* or religious philosophising by him whose mind and body have been purified and perfected by *Sādhanā*.

The Shaktisanggama Tantra says that the doctrine of *Shakti* was promulgated to establish unity amongst worshippers. For whatever might be the name of the God of their particular form of worship, all admitted His "feminine" aspect as Power. A Bengali writer, now deceased, who is not so well known as he should be, namely Bhudeva Mukhyopādhyāya stated in one of his books (on what authority however I do not know) that Shākta teaching was also promulgated with the political aim of hardening the power of resistance in the Hindu to foreign aggression. However this may be the doctrine is in fact powerful and power-giving. It is not possible that those who truly realise that in their essential being they are the self-same Supreme Power which created the universe, or in actual contact therewith, can be ever weak. It has been said that it was Christianity which first told the individual man that he was of worth.

But how can that be, seeing that hundreds of years before the incarnation of the Christ the Rishi had said "That thou art". That is, man is not only of worth, but he is *Devālaya* or abode of the Divine Power itself. Life itself is a power which is weakened or increased in the individual as he has ability to resist, and to increase through faith in, and progressive realisation of, his essential oneness with, the enduring Whole, which, while timeless in itself, is represented in time by a principle of conservation within the limits of the life of an universe. Abundant life is needed for the successful undertaking of all human activity. How to gain it is the work of *Sādhanā*. But in rightly stressing the necessity of practice, it has sometimes been forgotten, in the reaction against "Dogma," that practice must be backed by a doctrine which supplies the reasons for it. I read for instance that auto-suggestion is now being practised by the mere repetition of the words "I am becoming better and better every day and in every way," and the like. But unless one believes this what is the use of saying it? Some appear to believe without reason but with good results.

But others will not believe this without having been given first a reason to show why such belief is well founded and will therefore have good result. Be they sound or not, Shākta doctrine does give its reasons when it says that the ultimate Reality and inner being of each self is the unlimited Whole (*Pūrna*) of which the individual is a contraction or form, deriving the limitation implied in all form by the operation of those Powers which are Mind and Matter and the function of which is to negate the Whole or Consciousness (*Nishedha-vyāpāra-rūpā Shaktih*) as Yogamuni finely says in his Commentary on Abhinava Gupta's Paramārthasāra. That Really Real is the Inner Self and unlimited Being of which life in Mind and Matter is a limited form. It is Hale or Whole. It is unbroken (*Akhanda*) Bliss of which all happiness in the world is a fragment. It is unlimited Power in itself as the Transcendent Will. Limited Power exists in the form of the individual wills of living forms and the physico-chemical powers of Matter.

But all these forms of contraction are due to, and take place in, Mind and Matter. The one Spirit, which is changeless Bliss, is the essential being of all these forms. From this it follows that each form may make contact with, and then realise, the whole, which is his own essential Self, which is Health itself, the Source, infinitely joyous, of all limited power and life—*Prāṇah prāṇasya* as the Upanishad says or the "Life of all lives"—with results all beneficial to itself. To understand this however it is necessary to know the nature of Mind and its operations and therefore the meaning of the old saying in the Upanishads "What a man thinks that he becomes". If this be doubted the answer is "try". If the objector refuses to try a system which promises particular results, he cannot complain that he has had no benefit from it. Just as in the West one finds advocates of the Cult of Power, so others, both here and there, are opposed to it because of its abuses. It is true that Power may be wrongly used but that need not be so. The objection is not to the Cult of Power (which is not the same thing as the Cult of material force) but the use of it when obtained. In the same way loose thinking makes a distinction between Might and Right as though Might was wrong. There is nothing necessarily wrong about Might. The true distinction is between Might in the service of Right and Might in the service of Wrong. In the same way objection has been taken to the Shākta doctrine because it teaches *Yoga* through Enjoyment or *Bhoga*, as distinct from *Yoga* by Renunciation which but very few are willing to try, and are still less capable of achieving if they did. *Bhoga* which is both Enjoyment, and Suffering is not limited, in the former case, to "Beer and Skittles" or to be more up-to-date "Cinema and Dancing Teas". It is a sound principle but, like everything else, susceptible of abuse by the sincere but weak on the one hand, and the hypocritical pretender on the other. It is an old doctrine in this line of thought that perfection can best be attained if each seeker of it perfects himself in all common human functions, and in his own particular avocation whatever it be. However humble it be let him only place himself, his life with all its functions and actions in relation with the Whole, when they acquire meaning and strength. The individual life is then lived in and with the Universal Life. But it must be known what Life is. To this question this volume attempts to give shortly the Indian answer.

What is called the "Philosophy of Life" and Doctrine of Power is now in vogue in the West. "New Thought" as it is called (so akin in some respects to Shākta doctrine) says "Within you is the Power". "Spiritual healing" is taught and practised by the followers of what is called "Christian Science" to whom man's mind is "mortal mind" and the world of matter is a kind of *Māyā*. Great changes are taking place in Psychology. The debt of Theosophy to India is well known as also (though in another sense) of India to Theosophy which re-called to the Indian the value of his cultural inheritance. In Medical science, Psycho-therapy is establishing itself. An American critic reviewing one of the books which I have published on Tantra Shāstra spoke of this Scripture as being "perhaps the most elaborate system of auto-suggestion in the world"—a fact which he did not consider to be to its credit—for auto-suggestion, in its Indian sense, was not understood by him.

All these western movements are further instances of the approximation, which is now taking place, of modern western and ancient Indian thought to which I have often referred, as in the first volume of this Series on "Reality". There is no reason however for any racial bumptiousness on either side. These doctrines and practices are based on notions which are it is true very old in India. They are the product of Ancient India, of that Great India which thought for itself and did not wait for cultural food of any kind to be spooned out to it by strangers. To-day it is the West which is great not only politically but in its intense original life, in its worship of Power and Beauty, in its Art, Science and Philosophy, and in its keen research and elaboration of fresh ideas. There, even the smallest peoples with no great past history are respected Selves. India has not yet recovered from the state which laid her open to the foreign invader. She is still learning how to say "I" which if it be said will be the starting point of her activities. This is not to deny the existence of great evils or that the present European civilization carries within it, like everything else, the seed of its death. Moreover, though I think the East has influenced the West, as the West the East, it is possible that similar ideas may have sprung up independently. If a theory has any truth in it, it may be discovered without help from any other. It is in respect of the absurdities of others that we more often require to wait for information. Probably no really new "Truth" is true. There is much truth in the Ancient Wisdom which is being *re*-presented to-day, sometimes with a richer content and in most cases with an objective proof which was previously wanting.

The Upanishads (some of which are more than 2,000 years old) teach the essentials of the lines of thought to which I have referred, such as that man's essential being is the one Spirit: that that being is pure Consciousness and Bliss of immeasurable power, that Mind and Matter are two of its powers and as such one with it, for power (*Shakti*) and the possessor of Power (*Shaktimān*) are one, that man makes himself what he is and he can make himself what he will; that (to use the words of the Chāndogya Upanishad) "what a man thinks that he becomes," that the Power is within, being known as the "Inner Controller" (*Antaryāmin*), that Mind is active and goes forth as a Ray to meet the excitations of matter, that it has power over matter, and may possess various *siddhis* such as moving matter without physical connection and others, and that mind can influence mind by telepathy and hypnotism (*Vashīkaranam*) and in other ways. The recent theory, for instance, of the American Dr. Abrams that there is vibration (*Spanda*) of the "ultimate" electric units of matter, that specific rates of vibration are associated with definite pathological conditions of the blood or tissue, and that these conditions may be cured by electric waves possessing a periodicity enabling them to control the vibrations of the disease from which the patient is suffering, is strongly reminiscent of the theory of *Mantra*, which by its sound-vibrations affects and regulates the psychical and physical sheaths. In a recent book by a Bengali author it is observed (not with approval for he rejects the Vedânta and adopts the notions of Modern Western Theism) that it appeared to him that "in these modern speculations the old philosophers seem to have been winning all along the line". He says: "An Indian may well feel proud that the speculations of his age-old philosophers so long ridiculed by Europeans are adopted by the newest science"; but he finds that it is "difficult to resist the smile which such speculations naturally give rise to". Let him not resist the smile. No one will begrudge him that, for smiles and laughter spell health, nor will he perhaps demur to the amusement of others for a reason quite contrary to his own. Naturally those Indians who do not think much of the religion and philosophy of their ancestors will be amused (though the kindly ones will be saddened) at the sight of those Europeans who (as they think) are picking up ancient Indian errors and putting them forward as new Western truths.

Others of a different way of thinking will likely be of opinion that if modern western scientific theories tend to square with ancient Indian teaching, then some case is made out for the latter.

But after all it does not matter who first said what. The question is—is it true and therefore useful—a question which we should approach without prejudice.

My friend Professor P. N. Mukhyopādhyāya has been good enough, at my request, to supply me with the valuable Appendix which will be found at the conclusion of this book which will be followed by two volumes, which I have prepared with his help, on *Shakti* as Mind and *Shakti* as Matter.

Puri J. W.
30th May, 1922.

THE WORLD AS POWER

POWER AS LIFE

(PRĀNASHAKTI)

I

> "*He said 'I am Life'*" (*Sahovācha Prāno'smi*). "*The Life of all lives*" (*Sa u prānasya prānah*) "*Adore Me who am Life.*" (*Prāno'smi, Mām upāsasva*).
>
> Kaushîtakî Up., 3—2; Kena-Up., 2.

IN the West, matter is commonly divided into that which is organised and unorganised, the former being called living, and the latter non-living, substance, "brute" "inert" and "dead" matter. As is so characteristic of Western Thought, emphasis is thus laid on difference and discontinuity, these being apparent. An absolute gulf was created between the two;—the greatest of all gulfs namely that between what is dead and what is alive. "Organisation"[1] means more or less systematic arrangement of relatively separate parts in a whole suited to fulfil any sort of function. According to the old meaning of the term "organic," an organic body is one, whether living or not, in which heterogeneous elements make up a composite whole. After Leibnitz two elements in the conception (that of composition of parts and of relation of means and end) are intimately connected and Kant welds them together in his definition of the organic, as that in which all the parts are reciprocally means and ends to one another and to the whole. Thus historically the identification of organic with the living comes last, and the term means that which has life whether animal or vegetable as opposed to inorganic or inanimate. Organism in biology means a discrete body of which the essential constituent is living protoplasm. The term originally indicated the recognition of organisation as essential to life and as opposite to unorganised or "dead" matter. An

---

[1] See Baldwin. Phil. Dict.

organism has the inherent principle of its own systematic process. It is thus common to speak of organised matter in connection with life. But all matter is now held to be in a state of organisation, that is systematic arrangement of relatively separate parts in a whole suited to fulfil any sort of function. It is said to be constituted of complicated structural elements, and the molecules and atoms are described in fact as miniature solar systems. The supposed, self-moving, electric units of these atoms constitute distinct structural arrangements, varying in number and position in the varied forms of so called elementary matter. And so it has been said[2] that "as soon as we lift the veil of appearances, matter so inert in its outward aspect is seen to possess an extremely complicated organisation and an intense life". So again mineral being is characterised by its beautifully geometrical crystalline form as the living being is characterised by its anatomical one. In short all matter, every thing which exists is organised. It is therefore not organisation but degree and

[2] Le Bon "Evolution of Matter".

nature of organisation which distinguishes so called living and non-living substance.

Nothing again is inert. According to Sāngkhya and Monistic Vedānta all matter is a compound of derivates from one primordial Substance—Energy called Prakriti and Māyā-shakti. This and its modes are in perpetual movement. For activity is the essential characteristic of the ultimate Substance-Energy. For this reason the Hindus call the world "*Jagat*" which means the "moving thing" because everything is in movement in changeless Spirit or Consciousness, just as in the phenomenal world all is moving here and there in the ethereal continuum. It is true that a common distinction, in ordinary parlance, exists between moving (*Chara*) and unmoving (*Achara*) things, but this refers to the appearance only of gross matter and even to living plants without locomotive movement. This notion of the inertness of matter was due to superficial observation of molar masses apparently at rest and set in motion by force from without. As above stated, according to the views now held, the ultimate particles of the atoms of matter are in constant movement and the atom itself is a reservoir of tremendous energy. It has therefore been rightly observed that the whole question of motion, as related to living and not-living being, requires re-statement in view of modern ideas of an ultra-physical nature relating to intra-atomic activities and to molecular movement.

There is no Indian equivalent of the phrase "dead" matter. The term "*Jada*" generally means anything without locomotive movement (*Achara*) a stationary thing. In this sense a plant may be *Jada* though there is movement in the plant itself. A moving thing (*Chara*) may be relatively *Jada*. Thus a man who is numbed with cold is said to be *Jadasada*. One is said to be in the state of *Jada* when he feels incapable or disinclined for physical or mental action. *Jada*[3] means without movement (*Nihspanda*) effortless (*Nirudyoga*). It also means unconscious (*Achetana*). But a thing which is *Achetana* is not necessarily and absolutely without consciousness. In fact

[3] See Prakritivāda Dict. of Ramakamala Vidyalangkāra.

nothing is that. Everything in Vedānta is a form of consciousness (*Chit*). Everything again, as regards its material body, is Māyā-shakti or the finitising principle, Creatrix of the world of forms or Power which in itself (*Svarūpa*) is Consciousness. Again Māyā-shakti as ground of appearance is constituted of three Gunas (*Trigunamayī*).[4] That is in everything there is the Factor *Sattva* (for the three *Gunas* or factors of the Natural Principle never exist apart from one another), and *Sattva* is that aspect of the Natural Principle which manifests Consciousness in any phenomenon, veiled though that Consciousness be in differing degrees. What then we call unconscious or as having the appearance of unconsciousness is only that in which Consciousness is most obscured to the finite observer. But there is nothing which does not manifest it in some degree. Thus the response of matter to stimuli is evidence of the *Sattva-guna* and of the *Chit* which it reflects. In popular language *Achetana* (unconscious) may be applied to man who is *Achetana* to some

[4] See "Reality" by the Author.

things and *Chetana* to others. What may be in one condition *Achetana* may be *Sachetana* (conscious) in another. Thus *Achetana* (unconscious) may be applied to a man who is not expert or quick about anything, incapable, worthless, in a state of fascination, dumb, blind, an idiot, any one who remains without action and effort.[5] How little a Hindu looks on anything as being absolutely dead, and how words are used in an analogical sense is illustrated by the case of an Orissan sculptor who told me that he was unable to make a statue I wanted out of an old stone which I gave him because it was "dead"; that is it had ceased to be able to be worked upon.

From a philosophical point of view then all is essentially unmoving Consciousness veiled in varying degree by continually moving Mind and Matter, most veiled in gross matter, and less and less veiled in plants, animals and man, who in Yoga becomes complete Consciousness and nothing else. Again the vehicle of mind and matter is the

[5] Dakshatā, Satvaratā, Akshamatā, Akarmanya Mohita, etc., see Prakritivāda Dict.

manifestation of the Power (Shakti) of Consciousness, that is Consciousness as Power. The term Consciousness must be understood not in its ordinary Western sense but as an approximate term for *Chit*.[6] All matter again is composed of Sattvaguna as well as of the other Gunas which are the principles of efficiency, and resistance or inertia in a phenomenon. There is no vehicle of Consciousness which is not in perpetual movement. There is no vehicle which does not in varying degree display Consciousness.

Neither then organisation, motion, nor consciousness are peculiar to living substance. Motion exists in both forms of substance, though it is what is called mechanical and determined in one, and apparently free and undetermined in the other. Organisation exists in both cases, though more and more complex in living substance. Consciousness is the essence of both, though so obscured in what is called inorganic matter that the latter is deemed unconscious. Yet even here

[6] See "Shakti and Shākta," by the author. Chapter on Chit-Shakti.

science corrects crude observation. Thus irritability was supposed to be a fundamental property of living substance. It is however now known that "non-living" matter reacts to external stimuli. Thus its reaction to acid is a spasm. For knowledge in this direction we are indebted, as all know, to experiments of the distinguished Indian scientist Sir Jagadish Bose. By taking as basis the fact that the most general and delicate sign in life is the electric response, he has shown that this electric response is the reaction of an obscured form of Consciousness in matter. He has thus shown by his ingenious experiments the fatigue of metals and its disappearance after rest and the action on these same metals of excitants, depressants and poisons.

Whilst it is of course true that self-conscious mind exists only in high manifestations of Life, it is also the fact that in the response which inorganic matter makes to external stimuli we see the most rudimentary form of that which when developed is called sentiency—a form of Consciousness. Matter is of extreme mobility and it has been said[7] "endowed with an unconscious sensibility which cannot be approached by the conscious sensibility of any being". The author cited adds "This sensibility of matter so contrary to what popular observation seems to indicate is becoming more and more familiar to physicists. This is why such an expression as the 'life of matter,' utterly meaningless twenty-five years ago, has come into common use. The study of mere matter yields ever increasing proof that it has properties which were formerly deemed the exclusive appanage of living beings. The analogies discovered are, it is likely, due to the fact that nature does not greatly vary her procedure, and constructs all beings from mineral to man with similar materials, whence they are endowed with common properties"

Then is the substance we call matter different in what is living and not living? The answer is in the negative. It is the same matter which is in living substance as in non-living substance. There are not two kinds of matter. The chemico-mechanical

[7] Le Bon "Evolution of Matter," 249 (1907).

school stand for the continuity of evolution between non-living and living substance. The Vitalists say that there is no difference as to matter, but that, when viewing life, we are in the presence of "something else" (not matter) in addition to what is found existing in non-living bodies. Nature in fact constructs all beings from mineral to man with similar materials. The difference exists in the manner they are worked up to display the Consciousness which is their essence. The greater the display of consciousness the more complex the structure.

The various "elements" of matter may by combination give birth to bodies of increasing complexity from the forms of inorganic matter to the compounds forming the tissues of living beings. A living being is made up of an aggregate of chemical compounds formed by the combination of a small number of elements[8] so associated as to compose molecular edifices

[8] The human body is about 75 per cent water, rest jelly and bones. The nerves and brain cells are 80 per cent or 85 per cent water. The Colloids are, it is said, the underlying fabric of many of the processes of life.

of very great mobility. A particularly complex but structureless homogeneous undifferentiated chemical substance known as Protoplasm[9] is the substance out of which all "living" things, whether Plants, Animals or Men, are formed. This elementary life-stuff possesses even in minute portions all the properties seen in the most complicated living structures such as assimilation, growth, contractility, sensitivity, reproduction. Of it is built up the cell, itself a complicated structure with its walls and nucleus. Inorganic forms constitute molecular edifices of small complexity in structure, whereas compounds elaborated within the tissues of living beings are admittedly extremely difficult of interpretation. So long as chemistry had only to study very simple mineral or organic compounds, elementary laws were sufficient, but closer examination showed that substances existed to which none of the known laws of

[9] Contains carbon hydrogen, oxygen nitrogen and a minute quantity of other elements notably phosphorus. It is however so complex chemically as to defy exact analysis. Moreover it is dead protoplasm of which chemistry speaks.

chemistry could be applied and these substances are just those which play a preponderating part in the phenomena of life. A great number of chemical compounds, of which the aggregate constitutes a living being, possess a structure and properties to which none of the old laws of chemistry are applicable. No formula can express their composition and no theory explains their properties. On them depend the majority of the phenomena of life. The viscid albuminoid Protoplasm, which is the fundamental substance of the cells, never appears to change, though by its presence it determines the most complicated chemical reactions. The writer [10] from whom we quote the above speaks of the chemical edifices which the humble cells perform comprise—operations not only the most skilful in the laboratories but many more skilful still which man is unable to imitate. By means unknown the cells construct complicated and varied compounds and decompose the most stable bodies. "All these operations so precise so admirably adapted to one purpose are *directed*

[10] See Le Bon. *Op. cit.*, 293—295.

by forces of which we have no conception *which act exactly as if they possessed a power of clairvoyance very superior to reason.* What they accomplish every moment of our existence is far above what can be realised by the most advanced science."

A living being is, as body, the aggregate of these cellular lives. What then is that which we call life, be it in the cells or the cellular aggregate, as the plant, animal, and man? What is it which constitutes the distinction between that we call life and non-living substance? For it must be admitted that there are obvious differences between the two, otherwise man would not have made the distinction. It is sometimes forgotten, in the desire to unify all things, that it is the characteristic of phenomenal Reality that it is made up of differences and apparent discontinuities. For it is only these which can constitute a world. If all were static and homogeneous there would be no world at all. Continuity only exists as regards the original Substance-Energy (Shakti) of which all apparent diversities and continuities are modes. Nevertheless, whilst admitting diversity, we may discern elements of sameness or correspondence which are the phenomenal indications of the unity of Creative Reality Itself.

Varying definitions have been given of Life such as " the special activity of organised beings " which tells us nothing. Life is generally defined as a process and we are told what Life does rather than what Life is.

Thus living substance is said to be that which is born, breathes, moves, assimilates, grows, adapts itself to environment, repairs and reproduces itself and dies. Whilst it is true that these are fundamental properties of living substance, it cannot be said that, at any rate all of them, are properties of what is popularly called " living substance " alone. Perhaps in some degree none are. To be born and to die are only particular ways of coming into and leaving a passing form of existence. We cannot equate the behaviour of bodies with that of artificial machines. Thus the atom of matter does not depend on external impulse for its movements. It is not provided from without with its gigantic store of energy which it carries within itself. It keeps itself going until it dissociates. This dissociation is the death of the atom for which there must have been, as regards any particular atom, a corresponding birth. Nor can we say that one is self-moved and not the other. In gross matter there is intra-atomic and molecular movements, though as a mass it is moved only by the application of external force. "Brownian" movement may be a reaction of external molecular conditions upon a small mass of matter, resulting in mechanical motions, but it is yet a movement of transport. Even so called "self-initiated" animal movement may be a reaction to external conditions. Some are of opinion that there is no spontaneous or voluntary movement and that all movement is the result of tactisms in the nature of a chemico-physical reaction.

Then what of the admittedly living cell. Except as an independent organism it may be incapable of movement of transport. Thus only the white cells of the blood have amæbic movement. Some cells have ciliary movement only. Others, such as the living cells, have no movement of transport at all. These cells are yet living and form part of a living organism. All admittedly living substance breathes. And hence the word *Prāni* or breathing creatures. The plant does so through its leaves. Even in an animal, the Amæbə, we cannot see the process of respiration taking place. It is therefore supposed that the interchange of gases which constitutes the breathing process takes place all over the surface of the creature, there being no apparent special organ. It may not be too fanciful to suppose that some such interchange takes place, through attraction and repulsion, (principles of universal operation) in the interstices of matter. Whether " non-living " matter can assimilate depends on the question whether it is capable of growth. The process is in some measure chemical, for chemical changes and operations take place during its progress. All matter is capable of crystallisation, and matter is thus individualised by incorporation of elements borrowed from the medium with itself. Cells and crystals have been said to show evident affiliation. The crystalline form corresponds to the anatomical one. The material molecules go through successive transformations to assume the crystalline form, being a representation, in a way, of tissue in the course of evolution. All this of course is not to deny that there are differences between the growth of crystals and of so called "living" bodies. So again with self-repair which is a mark of living substance. Like the animal or plant a mutilated crystal can repair its mutilation. In fact this healing or righting tendency is not merely present in individual bodies, but is an essential characteristic of the universe as a whole—an aspect of the universal Law or *Dharma* under which all abnormality, injury and wrong are in due time righted. So again as regards generation. In certain conditions liquids only crystallise if they have first received a crystalline germ. In other cases spontaneous crystallisation appears to be observed. The crystalline bodies which are produced by admitted vital activities are identical in composition and molecular structure with crystals of "inorganic" origin. Adaptation, that is meeting the various conditions with which any living being is confined, may ultimately be reduced to Attraction (*Rāga*) and Repulsion (*Dvesha*), and response to changes in environment, whether the reaction be due to mere chemical changes in the composition of a thing, or whether there is also an element of purposiveness in them. Matter responds by expansion to heat, and by contraction to cold under rigid law. Lower organisms are also largely subject to such law but as they rise in the scale of being the element of freedom manifests. In all cases a purpose is served; in some only is the organism conscious of it. All forms of Matter and Mind act according to their inherent *Sangskāras* or innate tendencies to realise their ends, though only in some bodies is that tendency presented as object to its consciousness. The form is adapted to the end of accomplishing what the organism is by nature fitted to accomplish. In some cases the action is the realisation of a chemico-physical law, in others by instinct, in some others again by conscious willing process.

Every centre acts according to the degree of freedom which evolution has accorded to it. It is in fact in *freedom* that we find the distinguishing characteristic of living substance. It cannot be said that either organic or inorganic matter is altogether free. For each form exists and operates according to the laws which govern it. Each has its normal behaviour or *Dharma*. But living matter shows increasing will and purposive action.

If we then examine the differences which exist between so called inorganic and organic matter, we find that they may be summed up in the generalised statement that living-matter is endowed, in greater and greater degree, with *freedom* and *individuality*. External control is never wholly absent but there is increasing freedom from it. Instead of a rule imposed on simply-organised subject material, the forms of living matter are biologically described as an organism rich in organisation with internal self-regulating control. Chemical and physical processes are rigid and unvarying and a particular behaviour may be expected with accuracy. We do not anticipate any departure from the regular lines of events involved in any chemical or physical process. On the other hand an opponent of the Vitalistic theory[11] has said that an animal never does twice the same

[11] See Le Dantec "The Nature and Origin of Life".

thing in the whole course of its existence. Freedom and individuality is thus the fundamental characteristic of living matter. And this we might expect, seeing that the initial creative process is an impulse towards individualisation—an impulse which continues to gain strength with the evolution of forms.

The fact that gross matter exhibits (though in rudimentary form) the properties of living substance is regarded by some as proof that all matter is either, in an obscure sense, alive or has within it the potency of life. Either view is apt to introduce confusion and obliterate real differences. Life is a term which expresses a distinction. If we call all matter alive we thereby give to the word life a meaning which renders it meaningless. If again we say that matter as such contains the potency of life, we are again giving to the term matter another sense than that in which it is ordinarily understood, namely a sense which places it in contrast with both Life and Mind. The position taken by Shākta doctrine is in this matter, as in so many others, sound. It recognises both difference and unity. To the holders of chemico-mechanical theories of the production of Life by Matter, it says that Matter as such is not the cause of Life. On the contrary Life is a Power, a form of Consciousness which directs matter. But it is right to say that the cause of Life is immanent in matter as the Power which manifests as both Matter and Life. To the Vitalist, whether old or new, it says that he is right in affirming that Life is not a product of Matter as such, but wrong when he says that there is "something else" in living substance which is absent in non-living substance. For the one Power is present in both, but manifests either as so called "dead" matter with its regulated and calculable motions and behaviour, or in "live" matter in which the gradual freeing of consciousness and will introduces "self-initiated" purposive action which is less and less calculable, until for practical purposes it becomes incalculable. It is not in short to matter as such that we must look for the appearance of life, but to the Power (Shakti) which is the cause of *both* matter and life. This is so fundamental and important a point that it is examined later in greater detail, after a short historical review of the theories held in East and West as to the nature of Life and its so called origin.

According to the Indian materialists (Chārvakas, Lokāyatas) Life, as well as Consciousness, was spontaneously generated (Abiogenesis) as a result of the chemical combination, under the influence of heat and moisture, of the four kinds of matter [12] in organic forms, just as the intoxicating property of spirituous liquors is the result of the fermentation of unintoxicating rice and molasses. The instinctive movements of the newly-born organism were held to be mechanically due to external stimuli, as much as the opening and closing of the lotus at different hours of the day or night or the movement of iron under the influence of the lodestone. It is common ground however in the Nyāya-Vaisheshika, Sānkhya—Pātanjala and Vedānta schools that Consciousness [13] transcends and is not the product of matter. The Naiyāyikas held that

[12] Vāyu, Tejas, Ap, Prithivī. The fifth Akāsha was not admitted as not being subject of perception. See Seal, 239–91, Positive Sciences of the Hindus.

[13] Chaitanya. This is *not* mind. The latter is intermingled consciousness and unconsciousness.

psychical and vital processes are immaterial and could not be resolved into motion.[14] The two latter schools held that both Mind and Matter are, as all else, which is not consciousness[15], forms of motion, but are distinguished from one another in that the Vedānta holds that Life is also a separate substantive principle which the Sāngkhya, on the ground of economy of categories, does not admit. Both held that consciousness is not a motion and cannot be the resultant of the motions of inorganic matter. Nor is the consciousness of the self, or of the organism as a whole, the resultant of supposed consciousnesses vested in the constituent particles of the body. There is one central abiding Consciousness. Life[16] according to the Sāngkhya is not a *Vāyu*[17] or bio-mechanical force nor any mere mechanical impulsion resulting from the impulsion of

[14] Parispanda. Life. It is a Guna, jīvanayoniyatna or activity of the Âtman.

[15] As either the Sāngkhyan Purusha or Vedântic Ātmā. Both are transcendent, immaterial, and at rest: all else moves.

[16] Seal, 241.

[17] Vâyu comes from the root Vā — to move.

Vāyu. Life is a reflex activity, a resultant of the various concurrent activities of the mind and senses.[18] This, it is said, explains the disturbing effect on the vitality of pleasurable and painful emotions. The Sāngkhyas accept the substantive existence of Mind[19] but resolve Life into a mere resultant activity of the mind and senses. Whilst therefore for them Life was not a bio-mechanical force nor evolved from inorganic matter[20] it was only a complex reflex activity resulting from the operations of the psycho-physical principles or forces in the organism. The Vedāntists[21] whilst agreeing with the Sāngkhyas that Life is neither a bio-mechanical force, nor the result of its operation, deny that it is merely the result of the concurrent sensori-motor, emotional, and apperceptive reactions of the organism. Life is prior to the senses, for it regulates the

[18] That is Ego (Ahangkâra), the emotional (Manah) and sensori-motor (Jnânendriya and Karmendriya) relations of the organism.

[19] Manas, as derived, co-ordinately with the Tanmâtra, from Ahangkâra or individualised Prakriti.

[20] Bhūta.

[21] Seal, *op. cit.*, 242.

development of the fertilised living ovum from which the senses subsequently develop. The sensations do not explain life. Moreover the deprivation of any one or more of the senses does not mean a deprivation of life. The Vedāntists therefore hold Life, which is called Prāna,[22] as a separate, substantive, quasi-material Principle, pervasive of the organism, which is not a gross natural force or material energy but a form of regulative activity or motion guiding such energy phenomenally and, as the western Scholastics said, immersed in Matter. In the Shākta system, everything which exists is a form of Supreme Power or Shakti which is in Itself Consciousness and manifests as Consciousness-unconsciousness.[23]

[22] This word comes from the root *An* "to breathe"+prefix Pra.

[23] Neither the 24 nor the 36 Tattvas give Life as a separate substantive Principle or Tattva, as does the Māyavāda scheme. Life is here, as in the Sàngkhya, merely a complex reflex activity resulting from the operation of the psycho-physical Principles. It is a form of the Supreme Power which produces them, though possibly (for the point is at present not clear) after the manner of the Sângkhya. That is Life as Cause is Power, though the mode by which it works may be that which the Sāngkhya indicates.

That Power is either of Will, Knowledge or Action. The Life Principle is a form of active power (*Kriyā-shakti*). But the Powers are never entirely separated the one from the other. Wherever there is the one, there is the other. In particular manifestations, one or other may be predominant[24] Therefore there is present both Will and Knowledge and all these are manifestations of the one Consciousness. The Vital Principle is ultimately as all else Consciousness, in this case active to produce and sustain living substance and all its functions. Living substance is a form of God as Power.

Prāna has been defined[25] to be "the special relation of the *Ātmā* with a certain form of matter which by this relation the *Ātmā*[26] (or Self) organises or builds up as a means of having experience". *Prāna* in its general

[24] Pradhāna.

[25] "Hindu Realism," J. C. Chatterjee. In the Tantras the Devi as Life-Principle is depicted of a red colour in a boat floating on a sea of blood.

[26] This term is compounded of A+at+man. The root *At* means All-spreading just as Brahman does. According to some the root is As "to be" (Asmi, Sum, I am) or *An* to breathe—the "Spirit," which has the same significance.

sense as the "Life Principle" is not breath, nor is it breathing except in a secondary sense. Breathing is only one of the manifestations of Life, an attribute of living substance. It is a manifestation of the Life-Principle. Breath is simply the circumambient air inhaled and expelled. The form of the Life-Principle or *Prāna*, as manifested function, is breathing. Life, as the vital principle, bears the same name as its chief characteristic—the breathing which, in various forms, is the mark of vegetable, animal, and human nature. And thus the word "Spirit" literally means breath. Man must speak in terms of material existence, and he here selected what seemed to him the least material, the most unsubstantial. A breath may be felt. The physical action of breathing may be seen and known. When breathing ceases Life ceases: and so the Kaushitakī Upanishad calls *Prāna* "the Life-duration of all". But That which is unseen, of which its functioning is seen, is Spirit or Brahman as the Life and source of all lives, the *Prāna* of all *Prānas*.

Prāna is either individual or cosmic. The atter is the Brahman as *Prāna*. The special relation, above mentioned, constitutes the individual *Prāna* in the individual body. The individual *Prāna* is limited to the particular body which it vitalises, and is a manifestation in all breathing creatures called *Prānī* of the life-giving activity of the Brahman. The cosmic *Prāna* which pervades and vitalises all breathing creatures (*Prānī*) is the Brahman as the collectivity of all individual *Prānas*, and the source of the individual and collective life. Breathing is a microcosmic manifestation of the macrocosmic Rhythm to which the whole universe moves and according to which it appears and disappears. And so it is said that the life of Brahmā, the Creative-consciousness in any universe, is of the duration of the outgoing breath,[27] of the Lord as Time.[28] With His inbreathing all worlds are withdrawn.

The body is divided by the Vedānta into five sheaths, which are less and less gross as we proceed inward, namely the sheaths of food or matter, life, lower and higher mind

[27] Nishvâsa.

[28] Kâla—See Introd. Prapanchasâra Tantra, Vol. 3. Tantrik Texts.

and of bliss.[29] The *Prānamaya* or life-body differs from the gross outer body or body of food [30] which it vitalises. The latter is heterogeneous,[31] or made up of distinct or well defined parts. But the vital—self [32] which lies within the gross physical self [30] is an homogeneous undivided whole,[33] permeating the whole physical body.[34] It is not cut off into distinct regions,[35] as is the microcosmic cosmic physical body known as the Pinda. Unlike the latter it has no specialised organs each discharging a special function. It is an homogeneous unity, present in every part of the body which it ensouls as its inner vital self. A new life appears with the germination of the seed [36] in breathing creatures. Into

---

[29] Annamaya, Prānamaya, Manomaya, Vijnānamaya, Ānandamaya.

[30] Annamaya.

[31] Parichchhinna.

[32] Prānamaya Ātmā.

[33] Sādhārana.

[34] Sarvapindavyâpin.

[35] Asâdhārana.

[36] In the viviparous Placental (no a-placental animals were known) or Jarāyuja, the oviparous animals or Andaja, vegetable organisms or Udvijja.

this seed *Prāna* enters. When the *Prāna* goes, that is when the organism ceases to breathe, the organism which the Vital Principle holds together disintegrates, though for a time the cells may continue a sort of life of their own.

Prāna is metaphorically called *Vāyu* in the sense of universal vital activity. It is itself one, but on entry into each body manifests itself in ten different ways under ten different names, of which the five chief are *Prāna*, *Apāna*, *Samāna*, *Vyāna* and *Udāna* later explained.

Prāna or *Āyuh*[37] (Life) like all other constitutive principles of the Universe has two aspects namely as cause and as effect. In the first Prāna is a name for the Supreme Brahman as the Cause of, that is the Power

It was commonly believed that the fourth class Svedaja or Usmaja were spontaneously or a-sexually generated from inorganic matter through the action of moisture and heat such as maggots in corrupting flesh. See Rāghava Bhatta Comm. on Shāradā Tilaka, 1, 27, 29. But the view was also taken that inorganic matter without seed (Bīja) could not give rise to animal life. See Seal, *Op. cit.*, 177, 181.

[37] Āyuh is Prāna. Kaushītaki-Up., 3—2.

(Shakti) which produces, the life of individual being. Numerous Texts establish this: "He said 'I am *Prāna*' (*Prāno'smi*)[38] "Thou art *Āyuh*" (*Āyustvam*)[39] "*Prāna* is Brahman" (*Prāno brahma*).[40] Here *Prāna* means Parabrahman[41] beyond Mind and Speech.[42] Hence God is enjoined to be worshipped as Life. "Adore Me who am Life (*Āyuh*) and Eternal."[43] "He who worships Me as Life and Immortality obtains in this world all Life (*Āyuh*)."[44] Worship of life is done with life.[45]

[38] Kaushītakī-Up., 3—2: Prâna is Brahman (Prâno Brahmeti). *Ib.* 2—1.

[39] Maitri-Up., 5—1.

[40] Chhândogya-Up., 4—10—5. Kaushītakī, 2—1, 2—2.

[41] Brihadâranyaka-Up., 4—1—3.

[42] Kaushītakī-Up., 2—2. Here Prâna is indicative (Lakshanârtha) only. As the Parabrahmasvarūpa or transcendental Brahman *It* is beyond Prâna. Cf. "Thou art He who is other than Prâna and the Devatâs and Who art both." Kaushītakī-Up., 1—6.

[43] Kaushītakī-Up., 3—2 (He who is Prajnâtmâ).

[44] *Ib.* Cf. "They get life (Âyuh) who worship Brahman as Prâna." Taittirīya-Up., 2—3—1. Prâna is the third Pâda of the Gâyatrī, Taitt. 1—5—3.

[45] "I do Tarpana of Âyuh with Âyuh." Shiro-Up., 1.

It is this Prāna, as the Supreme Cause, which gives life as Effect.[46] He is thus the Life of all lives."[47] The Kānva[48] says "The Devas worship that which is the Deathless One (*Amrita*), which is truly Itself Life, and the Light of Lights."[49] The Āgama also says "As we two (Shiva and Shakti) are the Self of the World,[50] We Two are one with it. By reason of Our oneness with one another we are at all times the Life of the World (*Jagatprāna*)".[51] What is vitalised is so vitalised by Prāna.[52] And He is the Vitaliser or *Prāna* in chief.[53]

It is from this Supreme Life that all beings issue, enjoy their individual lives, and then re-enter into it.[54] It is thus the Cause of the

[46] Prānah prānāya dadāti, Chh.-Up., 7—15.

[47] Sa u prānasya prānah. Kena.-Up., 2.

[48] One of the recensions of the Brihad.-Up.

[49] Cited in Comm. to v. 1 to Kāmakalāvilāsa.

[50] Jagadātmatvāt.

[51] Cited by Natanāndanātha in Comm. to v. 12 of Kāmakalāvilāsa.

[52] Prānena abhiprānitah. Ait.-Up., 3—11.

[53] Mukhyah Prānah. Chh.-Up., 1—2—3; 1—5—3. Prāna is the fourth Pāda of Brahman. Chh.-Up., 3—18—4.

[54] Chh.-Up., 1—11—5. Prāna is Ra because in Prāna all beings enjoy (Ramante) Br.-Up., 5—12—1.

universe. As such, Life is eternal.[55] It is also this universe.[56] As Life eternal it is an endless, constant and changeless Persistence itself. It is also eternal as universe, in the sense that, whilst particular systems come and go, the universal process is eternal—now dropped and now resumed. *Prāna* is *Paramātmā*, *Antarātmā*,[57] that is Supreme Being beyond and in bodies as their Controller and Director. It is *Kāla* the force which urges on all things and is viewed as Time[58] "Fire" (*Agni*) (which is the builder of forms);[59] exhibited in matter,[60] though itself beyond matter.[61] Eternal Life is the persistent and true[62] which is enshrined by all name and form.[63] It is

[55] Prâno vâ amritam. Br.-Up., 1—6—3.

[56] Prâno 'sau lokah. Br.-Up., 1—5—4.

[57] Maitri-Up., 6—9, 6—1, 6—8 and 7—7.

[58] Maitri-Up., 4—5.

[59] *Ibid.*, 6—9. It (as Brahman) is Tejomaya. Br.-Up., 2—5—4.

[60] *Ibid.*, 6—11.

[61] It is Amritamaya. Br.-Up., 2—5—4 and Adhyâtma, that is above Daiva and Bhûta. Prâno vâ amritam. Br.-Up., 1—6—3.

[62] Prâna vai satyam. Br.-Up., 2—1—20.

[63] *Ib.*, 1—6—3.

formless.[64] All have form but It.[65] The Supreme Brahman is formless, and so also is the organising principle of bodies, though it takes on the forms of the matter in which it is immersed.[66]

Life then, in its causal sense, is a name for the Supreme Power (*Shakti*) in its aspect as the originator of individual lives. That Power is in itself Consciousness (*Chit*). This consciousness is immersed in matter and is there veiled and appears as the director, guide, regulator, and controller of its material energies.

It is not "material" in the English sense, that is, it is not matter. On the contrary Life or *Prāna* is said to be so called "because it leads and guides (*Pranayanāt*) and moves about."[67] Leads and guides what? The answer

[64] Atha amūrtam prānah. Br.-Up., 2—3—5.

[65] *Ibid.*, 2—3—4. Idam eva mūrtam yad anyat Prānāt.

[66] Vāyu, by which name Prāna is metaphorically called (in so far as Vāyu is a form of gross material Energy which Prāna is not) belongs to the formless (Amūrta) division of the Bhūtas (sensible matter).

[67] Pranayanāt prakramanāt prāna iti abhigīyate. (Prakritivāda Dict.). The first word may also mean because it builds up (matter) which is also a function of Life.

is Matter; for this which is the last product of the involution of Consciousness cannot, as such, guide and direct itself. The Vedānta clearly distinguishes, in its doctrine of the sheaths (*Koshas*) of the Spirit, Matter which is the outermost and most gross sheath, from the vital body which is the next inner and more subtle sheath, within which again are the sheaths of lower and higher mind and within the last the Self. The gross body is the sheath of matter or food [68], and within it is the vital or Prānic sheath [69] which, with Mind, are the subtle body of the Self. This latter is Consciousness, and Mind, Life, and Body are forms of its Power (*Shakti*).

If it be remembered that all is in essence Consciousness, veiled in varying degree by its Power as Mind and Matter, the nature of Life will be clearly understood. In the higher mind [70] functioning as Reason, Judgment and so forth, Consciousness is least veiled and most aware of itself. The lower mind [71] which

---

[68] Annamaya Kosha.

[69] Prānamaya Kosha.

[70] Vijnānamaya Kosha.

[71] Manas of the Manomaya Kosha.

attends directs and synthetises the functioning of the senses is more veiled. Animal instinct again is a veiled form of consciousness. Another form of the mental principle is *Prāna* or Life. Though not specifically called mind, it is nevertheless that aspect of mind which is wholly immersed in matter as the *directing* consciousness of the material energies of the body. For to limit, regulate, control in whatsoever way is the function of the mental principle, and that which is the patient of such operation is Matter. Consciousness is present and at work in all matter, whether we call it living or not living; but when it directs the material energies in such a way as to build up and sustain breathing creatures (*Prānī*) it is called *Prāna* or the Vital Principle or Force. And so the Maitrī-Upanishad [72] sums up these relations in the statement that the Life-Principle is the essence of Matter (and of food, which is matter which sustains life), the Lower Mind is the essence of the Life Principle, the Higher Mind is the essence of the lower mind, whilst the Self in its

[72] Maitri-Up., 6—13.

body of Bliss is the essence of the Higher Mind.[73]

The Vital Principle manifests itself in various functions. All movement in matter may be reduced to the centripetal and centrifugal, attraction and repulsion, which are psychically, like (*Rāga*) and dislike (*Dvesha*) and physically cohesion and affinity on the one hand, and their opposites on the other. Cohesion which links together the elements of bodies manifests in the mutual actions of the molecules. Affinity operates between particles of different bodies determining the majority of chemical reactions. Gravitation is an immense form of attraction and volcanic action is a repulsion on a large scale. In osmotic phenomena,[74] molecular attraction and repulsion are most clearly shown, there being produced two currents in a converse direction called exosmose and endosmose. These simple molecular attractions and repulsions, acting in the

[73] Prāno vâ annasya raso, manah prānasya, vijnānam manasah, ânandam vijnānasya.

[74] All substances which possess the property of dissolving in a liquid attract the solvent and are conversely attracted by it.

bosom of liquids, govern a great number of vital phenomena and are, it has been said, perhaps one of the most important causes of the formation of living beings. All such attractions and repulsions can act only at a certain distance. The term "Field of Force" is given to the space in which they are exercised and that of "Lines of Force" to the directions in which are produced the attracting and repelling effects.

Prāna, as a general term for Life, manifests in various ways and is thus given various names according to the functions.[75] *Prāna* is also the name of the chief of these functions. *Prāna* in the latter sense is the specific vital function which is *appropriation* or *injection*. It is the vital representative of the *centripetal* movement of matter and of the psychical principle which is Like or Attraction or *Rāga*. Leading instances of appropriation or injection are inspiration,[76] swallowing food or drink, absorption by the

[75] The chief of these are five and so in Prānāgnihotra Up., 2. Prāna = Agni = Paramātmā surrounded by the five Vāyus—Prāna, Apāna, Samāna, Vyāna, Udāna.

[76] Shvāsa. See Brihad.-Up., 1—3—7; 5—14—3.

skin, either naturally, or in the case of medication, by skin absorption. On the macrocosmic scale *Prāna* is gravity. Commonly *Prānavāyu*[77] is said to include the outgoing breath.[78] But treating *Prānavāyu* as appropriation and injection, it would seem properly to come under the next head or *Apāna*.

The latter is the specific vital function which is *ejection*, the vital representative of *centrifugal* movement in matter and of the psychical principle which is *Dvesha*, or repulsion and dislike. The organism appropriates and injects what it likes and wants and by ejection or excretion gets rid of what is not needed. It is instanced by all forms of elimination, and expulsion such as defecation, urination, sweating, nasal and aural excretion, semination, parturition. Thus in the last case the seed is received in the womb by *Prānavāyu* and is expelled as the child by *Apānavāyu*. On the macrocosmic scale we see

[77] Vâyu which comes from the root Vā=to move is here moving vital force in the form of Prāna. So also with Apānavâyu and the rest.

[78] Nishvâsa, as in Yājnavalkya where Prāna is described as Shvâsanishvâsarūpa.

it in operation in volcanic eruptions and oozing of moisture from the rocks and the like. It would be possible to resolve all vital functions into these two—*Prāna* and *Apāna*, but with greater particularity, vital functions are classified under three additional classes.

The third *Vāyu* is *Samāna*, the function of which is *assimilation*. By this food is selected and rejected, broken up, metamorphosed in digestion and then assimilated.

Vyāna is in general terms the function of *distribution*. What has been appropriated by *Prāna* and is not subject of ejection by *Apāna*; what has been assimilated by *Samāna*, is distributed by *Vyāna*. It includes conveyance of fluid blood produced from digested food, as also bodily movements as a whole, such as jumping throwing and any function not included in the foregoing or the next.

Udānavāyu is concerned in the exhibition of *voice-function*, utterance as talking, singing, shouting, utilising for this purpose the air inhaled by *Prāna*.[79] It is to be here observed that the physical air inbreathed is not *Prāna*

[79] See generally Charaka (Shārīrakasthāna, 1—3). Sushruta, Chakradatta, Shivasanghitā, Jnānasangkalinī Tantra and Gaurīkānjalikā Tantra, Shāradā Tilaka with Rāghava Bhatta's Comm., 1—45.

nor is the breath expired *Prāna.* Prānavāyu is the vital function by which the air is indrawn.

Five subsidiary Vāyus are also enumerated, concerned in the functions of belching, eyelid movement, hungering and thirsting, yawning and hiccup,[80] the last of which is a tonic contraction or spasm which takes place if there is no corresponding expansion and may perhaps be also identified with the *rigor mortis.*[81] Besides these gross Vāyus there are others, the Yoga Shāstra speaking of forty-nine.

The term Prāna is used also in a general way as being speech;[82] vitality in the limbs,[83] offspring,[84] the principle of movement,[85]

[80] Nāga, Kūrma, Krikara, Devadatta, Dhananjaya. To these some add others.

[81] It is said not to leave the body even after death. On this account apparently it is called Laukika Vāyu (Rāghava Bhatta, Comm. on Shāradā, 1--45) as it remains in the body when all the other vital forces have abandoned it.

[82] Br.-Up., 1--3--27.

[83] *Ib.*, 1--3--19.

[84] *Ib.*, 1--4--17.

[85] Vāyu, as in Brihad.-Up., 1—1--1. Vātah prānah; where it is said to be the third part of Purusha, the other two being Fire (*Agni*) and Water (*Jala*), these three being the Doshas of the body in the Vaidya Shāstra. See also Mundaka Up., 2—1--4, Mahānārāyana Up., 14--1.

food,[86] and the Sun which is the material source of all earthly life.[87]

The abovementioned special vital functions have each a centre of operation which centres are commonly said to be, as regards the first five principal *Vāyus*, in the throat (*Udāna*), heart (*Prāna*), navel (*Samāna*), anus (*Apāna*), and the whole body (*Vyāna*). It is however a mistake to identify the seats of these vital forces with these gross physical bodily regions. What is thereby indicated are the five subtle centres or Chakras in the spinal column called Vishuddha, Anāhata, Manipūra, Svādhishthāna and Mūlādhāra of which the Tattvas are "Ether," "Air," "Fire," "Water" and "Earth," respectively, these being names for various motions and densities of matter.[88] Thus, in utterance, the physical throat is involved but

[86] Maitri Up., 6—13. By food Prāna and by Prāna strength; by the Prānas Manas: Mahānārāyana-Up., 23—1. Anna is both food and matter.

[87] Āditya is Prāna. Prashna-Up., 1—5; it is the outer Prāna (Vahih prāna), *Ib.*, 3—8.

[88] See A. Avalon's "Serpent Power". These are the five physical centres. We are not here concerned with the sixth or mental Ājnā chakra. The words "ether" "air" are not to be understood in the English sense of the terms. See *Op. cit.*

the subtle vital centre is in the spine. The physical heart is merely a pumping machine, not directly concerned in breathing, though energy expended in utterance may affect the cardiac movements. The navel has nothing to do with assimilation, the centre of which is at that portion of the spine which passes through the navel region. *Apāna* is not in the physical anus but in the Svādhishthāna Chakra in the lower part of the spinal column. *Vyāna* is said to be " in the whole body " in the sense that its operation is over the whole body, from its seat in the lowest spinal centre the Mūlādhāra. The production of the *Jīva* is from this centre, though the process of reproduction namely semination is from the urethra governed by the Svādhishthāna tract.[89]

The Tantras, on the Yoga side, give the colours of the several vital forces observable by Yogic vision.[90] These colours are (following

[89] As regards the minor Vāyus, Nàga, Kùrma, Krikara, Devadatta, Dhananjaya, their places are given in Râghavabhatta, Comm. to vv. 44, 45 of Ch. I Shāradātilaka.

[90] Yogadrishti. Prāna Tattva is in Vedānta derived collectively from the Rajas or activity—aspect of the Tanmātras or infra-sensible " matter " one of such Tanmātras being colour and form. All Tanmātras

the order of the *Prāṇavāyus* given) emerald (*Prāna*) red like evening sun (*Apāna*) milky (*Samāna*) white like Dhatūrā flower (*Vyāna*) colour of fire and lightning (*Udāna*).[91]

It has been observed that the Yoga Shāstra speaks of forty-nine *Vāyus*. The Six Chakras are seats of the Letters and Tattvas or Principles of Mind and Matter. The sixth is the subtle psychic centre, and the remaining are subtle centres of physical function. It is clear that the first is more subtle than the remaining five. It is also clear that these five are less and less subtle between themselves as descent is made from the fifth to the first centre or Chakra, for they are the seats of Ākāsha, Vāyu, Agni, Ap and Prithivī, the five forms of movement which go to make up sensible matter perceived by the five senses. Each of these is more material or gross than that which preceded it. This greater materialisation as we descend is due to the increase of

---

except the first two are with form (Mūrta). Prāna is a form of Kriyā Shakti.

[91] The colours of the subsidiary Vāyus are dark cloud (Nāga) collyrium black (Kūrma) scarlet like the China rose (Krikara) white like crystal (Devadatta), white like Dhustūra flower (Dhananjaya).

Tamas or Mass. The pulse of movement slows with each increase of Mass and thus the highest number of vibrations is in the highest centre and these gradually decrease until the last or "Earth" centre is reached. In each of these centres there are certain letters, 50 in number if we include Ksha, in the Ajna or psychical centre, or 49 if we exclude Ksha as being a letter compounded of two other letters (Ka and Sha) appearing in the subsequent series. The letters are themselves each forms of movement of varying intensity or rate of vibration of which we become sensible by reason of the *Dhvani* or Sound which is their revealer. Thus *Dhvani* is not the letter but its revealer[92] and is caused by the contact of the vocal organs and the surrounding air producing sound-waves in it. The letter (Varna) itself is eternal[93] movement, which is known as "the sound

[92] See "Garland of Letters" by the author.

[93] In this and other similar cases "eternal" means during the life period of each cosmic system; these being infinite it is eternal, though appearing and disappearing with the dissolution of the particular system. The true Eternal or Brahman does not appear and disappear.

which is not produced by the striking of things together" (*Anāhata Shabda*), and which is revealed as gross sound to the gross ear through *Dhvani*. The vibrations of the letters are the same as those of the *Tattva* of the centre in which they are—in fact the letter is the movement of the Tattva manifested to the Ear as Letter (*Varna*). For this reason, when, on a proper[94] initiation, a Mantra is given, if the disciple is, on examination, found to be constituted in such a way that any Tattva is in excess or deficient, then the Mantra of that Tattva is given to him with the instruction to repeat it, if in excess with the outbreathing (*Uchchhvāsa*), when so much of the *Tattva* is ejected, or if in deficiency with the inbreathing (*Shvāsa*), when so much of the *Tattva* is injected, a practice which proceeds on the lines that the Tattva and its Mantra are one and the same.[95] The object is to obtain an

[94] Apparently many, if not most, initiations mean nothing nowadays, owing to the ignorance and apathy of both Guru and disciple.

[95] The Bīja Mantra ends with the Anusvara breathing or the letter Ma (M) as in this the "Sun" of letters the Tattvas or Principles are considered to be in equipoise.

equipoise, as near as may be, of the Tattvas which are variously predominant in various bodies. At the same time *Prānāyāma* regulates the psychic movements (*Vritti*), for breathing and thinking-movements synchronise. The letters are distributed as follows, 2 (consonants), 16 (vowels), 12, 10, 6, 4 consonants in each of the Chakras respectively. After the first psychic centre the order of the five Prānas, relative to the Chakras, are, as stated, *Udāna* in the second, *Prāna* in the third, *Samāna* in the fourth, *Apāna* in the fifth, and *Vyāna* in the lowest or sixth. From this it follows that *Vyāna* should be (as is in fact the case) the grossest of the five *Vāyus*, and Udāna which is called the Supreme *Vāyu* is the most subtle, after of course the vibrations of the psychic centre which are more subtle than any of the vibrations and movements of physical functions. That these centres govern and regulate the vital functions assigned to them is obvious from the scheme. A matter however which requires enquiry is the answer to the query what is the significance of the number of the letters in each Chakra relative to the vital function governed by it. It will be observed that starting from the last Chakra the number of letters increases 2, 4, 2, 4. To perfect the above scheme it would apparently have to be shown that *Vyāna* had four forms of movement, manifested collectively or separately, in the functions assigned to it; *Apāna* had six and so on. There are thus 49 forms of vibration in which Vital Force exhibits itself and the Letters are Life-forces revealed to us by gross sound. In short the "Garland of Letters" represents all the Forces which go to the making of the universe made known to us as *Dhvani*, just as they are manifest to us in other ways through other senses. The above account will also explain why there can be such a thing as medical and spiritual treatment, by sound and Mantra. We treat disease by touch, as in massage, and medication through the skin; through the eye by colour,[96]

[96] The colour treatment has been tried for several diseases and the effect of various colours on the mind is well known.

by the tongue through medicine placed on it and gross drugging; by the nose through chloroform inhalation and olfaction generally. The influence of harmonious sound as Music is invariably acknowledged. In the Yoga-Shāstra lettered sound is operative also, since it stands for a movement which exists also in the constitution of the person sought to be affected thereby. *Ākāsha* is operative in Māntric treatment, *Vāyu* in electric treatment, *Tejas* in that by radium heat and light, *Ap* in Hydropathy, and *Prithivī* in drugging with solid and liquids. This last is the grossest form of medical treatment. How gross and unnatural then is the modern treatment (if it be in fact such) by injection into the body of vaccines, serum, colloid preparations and the like?

The appended diagram will more clearly explain the matters described in the Text. The spiraline coil which gradually contracts, as matter becomes more and more gross, is Kundalinī Shaktī.

Ajnā centre. (external) region (eyebrows)	Ha —— 	Ksha.	Psychic function or Antahkaranavritti
Vishuddha chakra (throat)		16 vowels	Udāna form of vital force (Utterance)
Anāhata chakra (heart)		12 consonants	Prāna form of vital force (Injection)
Manipūra chakra (stomach)		10 consonants	Samāna form of vital force (Assimilation)
Svādhishthāna chakra (genitals)		6 consonants	Apāna form of vital force (Ejection)
Mūlādhāra chakra (Perinaeum)		4 consonants — 49	Vyāna form of vital force (Distribution)

The Āyurveda and other medical Shāstras treat of three Forces in the organism called Vāta or Vāyu, Pitta, Kapha usually translated as " Air," " Bile " and " Phlegm " over which some merriment is made, as over so many other things by the non-understanding. The gross or physical body is composed of five forces and the forms of material substance which they constitute. The first of these five is Ākāsha or Ether, though the former term is not to be altogether identified as is sometimes done with the Western physical Ether. For the moment[97] it may be defined as the continuum in which the plurality of individual centres move. The last is Prithivī which is literally translated "Earth" but really means any matter in solid state. Āyurveda does not deal in this connection with Ether but with the centres which are interpenetrated by it, nor does it deal separately with Prithivī because, for its practical purposes, it regards both liquids and solids as solids. The remaining three are first Vâyu which is translated "Air". Many are under the error of supposing that the air we breathe is Vāyu. Air is composed of oxygen, nitrogen, carbon dioxide, vapour and various other things. It is not a gas or chemical compound, but a mechanical combination of various gases and floating matter in mechanical combination. It cannot be accurately defined, for the nature of air, in this sense, varies at different places. It is not the same in a town as in the country, nor in the country as at the seaside, nor in a

[97] I deal with the subject in "Shakti as Matter' (Bhūta Shakti).

valley as on a mountain height. Vāyu is not air but the *menstruum* in which air, the mechanical combination, exists and by which it is held together. Vāyu comes from the root *Vā* which means "to move" and is, in its primary sense, motivity. Possibly as a substance constituted by such motivity it may be electric fluid just as Ākāsha or Vyoma may in the gross plane be ethereal fluid.

In the body it is exhibited as nerve force and as also any kind of electro-motor or molecular force and is in fact the power whereby the other principles of the body move. For without it they are said to be "cripples". In short it is as Sushruta says the force which sets the whole organism in motion.[98] It is the principal factor which determines the genesis, continuance and disintegration of the living body. This Vāyu is classified according to its function as Prāna, Apāna and the rest above described with five subdivisions of each. The other two principles are Pitta which literally

[98] See Introduction by A. Avalon to Prapanchasāra Tantra, Vol. 3. Tantrik Texts and the English translation (published in Calcutta) of Sushruta Samhitā by Kavirāja Kunjalāla Bhishagratna.

means Bile and Kapha which literally means Phlegm. But these are not either, except under those conditions in which they are transformed into Malas or fit to be ejected; but they are not Bile and Phlegm in those planes of their functions which determine the genesis, growth and continuance of the organism as well as its death, decay, and disintegration.

The function of Pitta or Agni (Fire) is, amongst others, metabolism and the bodily heat which is the product of the latter. One of its important functions is digestion, metaplasia, and assimilation. There are said to be 5 chief "Fires"[99] in the body each again of four subdivisions[100] as in the case of the next Principle or Shleshmā. Kapha or Shleshmā which is similarly divided is Apa that is the moisture principle. The watery principle keeps in check the last. The equipoise of these principles is essential to health. If Heat (Pitta) predominates the body

[99] See *Ibid.*

[100] Thus Pāchaka Pitta which is digestive heat is divided into one digestive fire of the mouth, two digestive fires in the stomach namely peptic and hydrochloric acid and two in the intestine namely Pancreatic and Bile secretions.

dries up, if Moisture (Kapha) predominates heat is extinguished and if Motivity predominates there is irregularity everywhere. These three principles embrace the whole sphere of organic existence. These three principles are called Doshas[101] and Dushya is that which is affected.[102] All Life as movement arises under conditions of heat and moisture which as the manifestation of Divinity are the objects of worship in the Vedas.

There is as yet no general agreement on the fundamental problem of the nature of Instinct. Instinctive behaviour has been defined by Dr. Lloyd Morgan as that which is, on its first occurrence, independent of prior experience, which tends to the well-being of the individual and preservation of the race, and which is similarly performed by all the members of the same group of animals, and which may be subject to modification under the guidance of experience. Instinct is also not uncommonly described as race-habit.

---

[101] Literally Faults because of the diseases to which their disharmony leads.

[102] See Prapanchasāra 15, namely, the Dhātus or substances, skin, blood, fat, etc.

Instinct is an organised expression of what goes on in the unconscious. It is however now thought that animals are not altogether perfect in their instinctive functioning. Instinct is a Sangskāra or tendency and aptitude manifesting as vital Power in Prāna. On its first occurrence in any individual it is independent of prior experience as had in that particular form, but it does not actually then commence but is a tendency, now latent now patent, in the whole series of evolution to which the individual displaying instinct belongs. The behaviour of inorganic matter is apparently fixed and calculable and seems mechanical. This fixedness of behaviour though less rigid appears in living substance as instinct. But not only is there a relatively greater freedom but the instinct may become modified and from out this basis of instinctive action self-consciousness and self-directed movement arise.

Heat, light and moisture are the generating conditions of all life evolved by the life-giving principle. It is heat and moisture diffused throughout nature which fosters life in all its forms. This Heat and Moisture like all else exist in gross, subtle and causal form. Agni, Varuna and Soma are with others, names of the One—"That which is one the wise call it by various names."[103] When then it is said in Veda[104] that in the beginning there was the Causal Water in which the One developed by the power of, or out of, Tapas and Desire[105] reference is not made to material Heat but to that intensive creative brooding thought and will which projects the universe, in which one of its gross transformations is material Heat in many forms some subtle, some gross. Fire is seen in the heavenly bodies, flaming masses of molten viscous or earthy matter, in lightning which liberates a kind of light and heat[106] latent in the aqueous particles and vapours[107] just as the ordinary domestic and sacrificial fire[108] liberates it from wood or fuel.[108] Fire is

[103] Rig-Veda, I. 64.

[104] X. 129.

[105] Kàma that is Ichchhá or creative will.

[106] Tejas.

[107] Agni is "Son of the Waters". The lightning flashes from the celestial cloud-ocean.

[108] The flame of burning wood (Indhana) is not pure Tejas for there is chemical union with earth-particles acted on by energy when the light and heat

stored up in the igneous rocks and exists as the various stores of animal heat. There are thus said to be ten Agnis or fires in the body. [109] In short heat, light, moisture as everything else which is manifested are various modes of the motion or activity of the supreme source of all such activities or Power. For the Vedāntists resolve all activity, physical, vital, and psychical into modes of subtle cosmic motion. It is not however the heat or moisture which directly and alone generate life. They are merely the conditions under which Supreme Power as Prāna Shakti manifests itself. That Supreme Power is manifested. Whilst all manifestation is movement, whilst all manifestation is a transformation of one and the same material Cause, yet differing names are given to the differing manifested

particles latent therein come forth as flame. It is not that the fire which is seen is there unseen but the potential energy which, given the necessary conditions, manifests as the seen fire.

[109] Three are immanent in the Doshas and seven in the Dushyas (see Introd. Prapanchasāra Tantra, Vol. III, Tantrik Texts Ed., by A. Avalon). Pitta is fivefold, *viz.* Pāchaka, Ranjaka, Sādhaka, Ālochaka, Bhrājaka as also Kapha, *viz.*, Shleshmaka Kledaka, Bodhaka, Tarpaka, Avalambaka.

forms. These denote the functioning or Power. It is that Power which manifests as both organised and unorganised matter but the organisation of it is not by matter but by and as the Power Itself in Its aspect as the organiser of matter, to be the receptacle of all the grades of life. What then are these grades?

Given the fact that all beings and things have their origin in one and the same material cause of which they are transformations, it necessarily follows that all things are essentially and ultimately one. They are one as to the general Energy-Substance (*Shakti*) of which they are manifestations which Energy-Substance is active to reveal the static Reality as Mind or to obscure it as Matter. But this Energy or Power has various modes. These are the varied forms of it, displaying the generic and specific qualities of things. The qualities of things are modes of Power (*Shakti*) acting in these collocations. These forms appear according to an order or law of succession under conditions of causality, space, time and mode and hence in the world all effects do not manifest themselves at once. So-called inorganic matter and organic matter as vegetable or animal organisms[110] however differing as forms are thus essentially and ultimately one—in respect of their Substance-Energy. Metaphysical continuity is indicated in the graded continuity of forms.[111] At each stage of evolution there is a going forth (*Prasara*) of Power (Shakti) which stores up its Energy in some relatively stable form. There is then another push of Power to form a fresh equilibrium. These points of relatively stable equilibrium constitute stages in the evolutionary process. The redistribution of mass and energy which occurs at each of such stages constitute the various forms of chemical,

[110] Organic compounds are either vegetable (Sthāvara or Achara Bhūta or immoveables) or animal (Asthāvara or Chara or Jangama Bhūta). Both are compounded of the five forms of sensible matter (Bhūta) in greater or less proportions.

[111] See Seal *Op. cit.*, 17, 55. on the Sāngkhya citing Pātanjala Sūtras and Vyāsa Bhāshya. So it is said Jalabhūmyoh parināmikam rasādivaishvarūpam sthāvareshu drishtam. Tathā sthāvarānām jangameshu jangamānām sthāvareshu (the evolved properties of Rasa and the like are seen in immoveables that is vegetables. And these properties of immoveables or vegetables are seen in animals and these properties of animals are seen in vegetables that is immoveables).

vegetable and animal species. There is no matterless mind nor mindless matter. The question is whether (the Cause, being transformed into inorganic matter), the power to organise the latter so as to display the phenomena of life comes directly from the inherent power of the effect as such, or must be attributed to the Cause as a special form of functioning which is Prāna or the Life Principle. All change is transformation of Energy due to collocations of the threefold tendencies of the material cause in its varied products. The potential energies of infra-sensible matter[112] are actualised as the five forms of gross sensible matter.[113] The latter is a compound of the former and undergoes a change of state. From the five forms, compound substances are made and so the variety of all substances in the world is produced. These material substances go to the up-building of the bodies of all forms of organic life. These show vital phenomena as birth, assimilation of food, growth, death, sentiency, waking and sleep, health, disease

---

[112] Tanmātra.
[113] Bhūta.

re-production, response and movement within limits.[114] Plants[115] have a sort of dormant or latent consciousness and are capable of pleasure and pain.[116] Chakrapâni in the Bhānumatī speaks of such consciousness as being of a stupified sort, that is darkened or comatose;[117] as also Udyāna who speaks of their very dull dormant consciousness.[118] In a well known passage from the Shāntiparva of the Mahābhārata, it is said that plants have a (rudimentary) sense of hearing, touch, sight, smell and taste.[119] They feel pleasure and pain

[114] Seal 169 where some authorities are given.

[115] See as to Hindu ideas concerning plants and plant life, Seal *Op. cit.*, 169.

[116] *Ib.* Antah-saṁjnā bhavantyete sukhaduhkha-samanvitāh (these have inner consciousness consisting of pleasure and pain).

[117] Vrikshâstu chetanâvanto'pi tamashchhannajnā-natayâ shâstropadesha-vishayâ eva. (Trees though possessed of consciousness by reason of their consciousness being overspread by Tamas are esteemed objects according to Shâstric teaching.)

[118] Atimandântahsaṁjnitayâ iti (because vested with a low degree of inner consciousness).

[119] The illustrations given are:

It is affected by thunder; it dries up under the touch of heat; the creeper finds its way and is therefore not eyeless; it drinks through its root and

and when cut down they die. "Therefore (it is said) I see Jīva, that is living organism, in it. There is no unconsciousness there."[120]

The next evolutionary stage (however brought about) is the lowest, lower, and then the higher forms of animal life and lastly man. The differences between plant and animal life have always been regarded by the Hindus as being one not of kind but degree.

Moisture and Heat are essential factors in the generation of all animated matter which is divided into four chief divisions of which the plant life is the first and lowest. It is born through moisture and heat[121] and is called Udbhijja that is that which "pierces up" from the ground such as grasses, creepers and other plant forms. These spring from seeds. Life-potentiality is not merely contained in the seed but in the seed and environing conditions. The animal seed is developed in the egg or in

knows whether water is healthy and has therefore taste. Various odours free it from disease so that it bears flowers and so it has sense of smell.

[120] Jīvam pashyâmi achaitanyam na vidyate.

[121] Svedaja or Ushmaja. "Heat" not "sweat" as some absurdly translate it.

the case of viviparous animals the mother's body. The mother's body, in the case of the plant-seed, is the earth, subject to the play of air, warmth and moisture.[122]

The next class is called Svedaja or Ushmaja, moisture or heat-born. These conditions are common to plant life and the following forms of animal life. It was supposed by some of the ancients both in the East and West that there was a sort of spontaneous generation of the lowest forms of life from moist and heated inorganic matter such as rotten wood and excreta. Not improbably the reason for this was the minute character of the seed or germ and lack of knowledge as regards generation by fissure or gemmation. The opinion however was also held that Svedaja animals must be included there under the oviparous or plant-seed class; the idea being that though vegetable organisms may pass off into animal there cannot be

[122] Rāghava Bhatta (Comm. on Shāradā Tilaka, I.27), says that when the earth is thus prepared it gets the state of "seedness" (Bījatva). The seed is planted and watered and then the seed attains the root-stage (Mūlabhāva) and then sprouts and continues to grow.

generation without seed[123], or ovum, and inorganic matter without either of these cannot give rise to animated matter in any form.[124]

The next division was the Andaja or oviparous animals and the highest and last the Jarāyuja the viviparous or placental. An ancient author's[125] classification is based on the number of senses possessed by animals, such number determining its place in the series. As none of the senses are wholly absent in any form of living matter, probably only well developed and active senses were alone intended; rudimentary or dormant senses being not reckoned. This classification has the advantage of distinguishing man from other mammalia which like him are viviparous by the former's possession of five well-developed and active senses and all the mental operations based thereon.

[123] Bīja.

[124] Seal *Op. cit.*, 181, citing Chhāndogya Upanishad. Prapāthaka 6. Part 3 and Shangkara Comm. on same where the classification of animals is on this basis of their Bīja, that is seed or ovum.

[125] Umasvati, the author of the Jaina work Tattvārthādhigama. Seal *Op. cit.*, 188.

The constituents of the physical body are called Dhātu, of which there are seven namely Chyle (Rasa) derived from food, Blood (Rakta) derived from chyle, Flesh (Māngsa) derived from blood, Fat (Meda) derived from flesh, Bone (Asthi) derived from fat, Marrow (Majjā) derived from bone, Seed (Shukra) derived from marrow.[126] The seed of woman is called Strī-shukra and sometimes Shonita—which in this connection does not mean menstrual blood which is Artava. All this development takes place by metaplasm or conversion of one tissue into another. By heat the Chyle becomes Blood which is built up into Flesh, and also by a reverse process it becomes Fat with its interstices in which, by deposit of calcium salt, the bone is formed. Marrow is formed by the tunnelling of the bones of the tissue of which it is the essence. Semen (Shukra) is the essence again of marrow and the most elaborated of the Dhātus, which

---

[126] In some cases Tvak (Skin), Roma (Hair), are stated in lieu of, or in addition to, those above stated. Thus Bhāskararāya in his commentary on the seventh Rich of Bhāvanopanishad speaks of nine Dhātus, *viz.*, those given in the Text and Roma and Tvak.

exists not merely in the testicles but is spread in subtle form throughout the whole body in the subtile channels known as the Shukravāhinī Nādīs, and is worked up into the gross form in which it is ejected in the genital organs.[127] The tissues of the developed seed in the male (Shukra) and female (Strīshukra) generates the child. Ojah is not one of the seven Dhātus but a substance which may be said to be the essence of all, which gives vitality to all and which "when it dies, man also wishes to die". It gives glow to the whole body. The Devatās of these seven Dhātus are Dākinī and others situated in the seven Chakras or centres.[128]

---

[127] The extraordinary use to which some so-called "Tantriks" put semen is founded on the theory that it is Soma which gives deathlessness in the physical body.

[128] Dākinī, Rākinī, Lākinī, Kākinī, Ṣākinī, Hākinī, Yākinī which according to the Mahāyoginī Nyāsa in the Saubhagya-ratnākara are protective Devatās over skin, blood, flesh, fat, bone, marrow, seed and all other Dhātus respectively situate in the Vishuddha, Anāhata, Manipūra, Svādhishthāna, Mūlādhāra, Ājnā, Sahasrāra respectively.

In the Shatchakranirūpana (Tantrik Texts, Vol. II) Dākinī, Rākinī, Kākinī, Ṣākinī are in Mūlādhāra, Svādhishthāna, Anahata, Vishuddha respectively, the other three being the same.

Three principles are at work in the body namely Pitta, Kapha, Vāta, the rendering of which as "Bile," "Phlegm" and "Air" gives no idea of their meaning. They represent the principles of Heat (Tejas) Moisture (Ap) and Activity (Vāta or Vâyu) respectively. The first two, when in excess manifest abnormal states of Bile and Phlegm which are excretions (Mala) of substance of which the body is ridding itself.

These three are called Doshas. Vāta is classified into Prāna, Apāna and so forth above mentioned. All metabolic processes are called Pitta, which has also five subdivisions according to functions and locations. Kapha or Shleshmā is also of five kinds, the functions of which are to supply to the body its watery element. Vâyu, Pitta and Kapha are thus fundamental principles of the human economy when, in virtue of their correlative and sustentative functions, they ensure an equipoise among the different vital and physiological processes essential to its health; for disease is a lack of harmony and of completeness. Hence the word "hale" which means "whole" When the equilibrium is disturbed, pathological conditions arise which form the *esse* of disease and then they are said to be transformed into Doshas or morbific diatheses. As excretions of Apāna Vāyu they are called Malas. Thus Vāyu, Pitta, Kapha are not "Air," "Bile," and "Phlegm" except under those circumstances in which they are transformed into Malas. They embrace both the biological and pathological principles of the organisms.[129]

The whole body is intersected by channels or Nādis which are both gross and visible as nerves and arteries, and also subtile and invisible to ordinary, but visible to yogic, vision. The "Eye of Food" is not the only one. Thus recent mention has been made [130] of the extraordinary capacity of a man to discern through the clothed body the existence of morbific growths in it. This is only an instance of the Siddhi of clairvoyance which it is claimed

[129] See my Introduction to Prapanchasāra Tantra, Vol. 3. Tantrik Texts and the Sushruta Sanghitā (English Trans.) Edited by Kavirāja Kunjalāla Bhishagratna. Like the old Western systems the Indian is a kind of "humoral" system.

[130] By Sir Conan Doyle in his "Wanderings of a Spiritualist," p 137.

laid bare to the Yogīs the numerous subtile channels though which the bodily Energy-Substance functions.[131]

In the highest man evolution on the material plane ends. Evolution takes place through the Power of God which as material cause is always transforming Itself into higher forms in order that Spirit may be freed of the bonds of Mind and Matter in which It has involved Itself. This is the Eternal Rhythm of the Divine Mother as Substance-Energy. He who "sees" that is creates Otherness resolves it into Herself again. That is His "Play" (Līlā). Those who enter into the spirit of it and follow its laws gather the fruits of the world. It is given to man alone to recognise the Player, to unite himself with Her and thus to free himself from the fields of play which are the eternally recurrent universes. The Devotee (Bhakta) of the Mother as She is in Herself—seeks not Her limited forms, but Her own unbounded Self. It is not life in forms that he wants, though he

[131] See as to these Yoga-Nādī, Avalon's "Serpent Power".

knows them to be the Mother-Power, but the Life of all Lives which is Her own Brahman-self. But there is also another form of Devotion, that is Devotion to Her as Form, as universe. Here too *Siddhi* of the so-called " lower form " is obtained when the form is recognised as Her form. For that recognition is itself strengthening of individual power. In Karma-yoga without attachment both ends and aims are served.

APPENDIX

LIFE AND THE FIRST PRINCIPLES

BY

PROFESSOR PRAMATHANATHA MUKHYOPÂDHYÂYA

LIKE many other terms such as 'Âkâsha,' 'Jyotih, etc., the term 'Prâṇa' is used in the Shruti to connote, in the ultimate sense, Brahman. The Vedânta discussing certain texts (see Vedânta, I. 1.23, I. 1.28, etc.) from the Chhândogya and Kaushītaki-brâhmaṇa attempts to establish this.

In fact, any Principle which exists and acts as adhiṣhthâna (ground) in relation to any bhūtas (created things) is a manifestation of Brahman.

Because the ground or Adhiṣhthâna is everywhere Brahman: the part is always grounded in the whole (Pūrṇa), the particulars in the general.

If, for example, X exist as the ground of the things A, B, C, then X, in so far as it is the ground, is a manifestation of Brahman which is the Ground Principle.

Now, Prâṇa even in the ordinary sense is the ground of the Indriyas. The Indriyas work so long as the Prâṇa is there in the body; they cease to exist when Prâṇa leaves the body. In *Sushupti* again, the sense-capacities are absorbed in the Prâṇa; in

Jāgrat they reappear out of it again. "Yadā vai puruṣhah svapiti prāṇang tarhi vāgapyeti prāṇang chakṣhuh prāṇang manah prāṇang shrotrang; sa yadā pravudhyate prāṇādevādhi punarjāyanta iti."

Hence, Prāṇa as the ground of the senses is a manifestation of the Ground Principle (*i.e.*, Brahman).

But Prāna in the ordinary sense is not the ultimate ground—the Pūrṇa itself. So that Brahman is spoken of as "Prāṇasya Prāṇah"—the Life of Life.

The matter may be stated otherwise:

The bodily functions including the sense-functions represent a stress-system (or system of acting and reacting forces).

Prāṇa is the root or ground of such functions; because without it they all cease.

Prāṇa is the radix of a particular stress-system.

The radix of stress-system considered as a whole is Brahman (as Chit).

Hence, Prāṇa is an aspect or manifestation of the Ultimate Radix (*i.e.*, Brahman).

The question, however, is this:

How does the ultimate Ground Principle become (or appear to become) an individualised or circumscribed Ground Principle? In other words, how does Prāṇasya Prāṇah appear as Prāṇa? If we know the process and its stages, we know the mutual relations of Mind, Life and Matter which are all aspects of the Ultimate Principle.

To understand this, let us begin by analysing our world of experience (*i.e.*, Fact).

World of experience = Chit involving Stress ('Stress' meaning Power to evolve or appear as a varied order of phenomena)=Chit (Sattva, Rajah, Tamah); S, R, T, being the three partials into which stress can be decomposed. Now, what is the nature of Chit considered as Chidākāsha (Ether of Consciousness)?

On reflection on the nature of this Ether of Consciousness. we find that it possesses three svarūpa lakṣhaṇas—*viz.*, unity, wholeness and freedom: It is Eka; It is Pūrṇa; It is Avādhita (*i.e.*, uncircumscribed, unrestricted). The whole Stress-system operates *in* this Ether.

Though the Ether as Chit never really loses Its nature (anyathābbhāva), it appears, by reason of the operation of the Stress-system (*i.e.*, S, R, T) in it, to move or change. As for example, the ākāsha which is contained or circumscribed by a jar *seems* to move from one place to another when the jar itself is moved.

Since, however, the Stress-system is really one with the Chit Itself, we may say that the latter has two aspects, *viz.*, static (Shiva) and moving or kinetic (Shakti); that is, Chit is kinetic (Shangkara, from the transcendental point of view, will say—*seems* to be kinetic) without ever ceasing to be static: Shakti must ever play on the breast of Shiva. The relation stated is alogical. To speak of 'aspects' of what is an indivisible unity is pictorial thinking. We cannot however help this if we must think and speak at all about the unthinkable and unspeakable Fact.

Let us consider the Motion-aspect. How can we state the Movement? Stress is resolved into three factors—S, R and T (Sattva, rajah, tamah). Movement of the Stress-system is its movement between the two limits, *viz.*, S (manifestation) and T (veiling). That is, the Stress-system moves from maximum veiling to maximum manifestation (or minimum veiling), and *vice versa.* Manifestation of what ?—Of the Essence.

The movement is rhythmic.

The movement of the world as a whole is rhythmic (alternate srişhti and laya); movement is rhythmic in the details also, *e.g.*, heavenly motions, seasons, etc., motions in the living cells and organisms, motions in the atoms, and so on.

To use a physical figure, the movement cannot be represented by a moving simple pendulum: it is rather spiraline, or coiling movement.

Since it is rhythmic also, the Stress-system is alternately coiled and uncoiled.

Movement, therefore, analysed gives us these two elements:

(1) A finitising process; (2) an uncoiling and coiling process (vikāsha and laya). By the former we have in the world an hierarchy of samaşhtis vyaşhtis (genera and species) having at the one end Ishvara as the *Summum Genus* and at the other the "point charges" or shakti-vindus which are the *infima species.*

On account of the existence of this hierarchy, we have a double set of world-derivates, *viz.*—a Samaşhti principle and its vyaşhti mode, *e.g.*, we have both Samaşhti manas and vyaşhti manas;

Samaṣhti p r ā ṇ a and vyaṣhti p r ā ṇ a. 'Samaṣhti' does not mean 'arithmetical sum total'

The two processes (finitising and coiling-uncoiling) are concurrent.

Now, let us treat the latter process—Evolution-Involution.

Evidently the process is a resultant of two tendencies—*viz.*, association and dissociation. In the case where the former tendency proponderates, we have this fact—*viz.*, a given point, A, more and more recedes from the centre X; this is uncoiling. Where the latter tendency is in excess, we have A more and more nearing X; this is coiling. Where the ratio of attraction to repulsion (Rāga to Dveṣha) is constant, we have simple rotation or revolution of A round X in a fixed orbit. Where the ratio is variable, we must have evidently either the coiling or the uncoiling diagram traced by the moving point. The two tendencies are opposite *saṅgskāras*; and their ratio is the *adriṣhta* of the given point A in relation to X.

In mathematical analysis we commonly regard the adriṣhta of a material body or particle (*e.g.*, the earth or the moon in the solar system; the electrons in the atomic system) as constant, because that assumption simplifies the data of calculation. But really a constant, unchanging adriṣhta is an abstraction, not fact. Adriṣhta being determined by the relative dispositions of S, R, T, must change, for it is the nature of these latter to always change. Hence, the simple rotatory motion of physics is an abstraction: it is obtained by limitation of the actual data. The earth, for example, is not *exactly* revolving round the sun, but moving in an eddying sort of motion. This eddying (coiling) movement may be clockwise or anti-clockwise. When the former, the earth may be gradually drawn towards the central solar mass, and be ultimately merged in it. That will mean the laya of Prithivī (*i.e.*, of the planet). When the latter, the earth may be gradually receding from the solar mass, in which case again, after a certain critical stage has been reached, the earth may be dismembered from the solar system, and drift into space. In both cases we have a *critical stage*. Suppose the earth is eddying round and round *towards* the Sun; after a certain critical stage has been reached, it will cease to go round and round, but will be pulled to the centre and merged in it; *vide* the career of a piece of straw in an eddy in water. In eddying *away* from the centre there is also a critical stage, after which the body ceases to eddy, but flies off from the circuit. Orthodox Astronomy will now hardly accept this account of celestial motion, but it should be borne in mind that spiral nebulæ have doubtless played a great part in cosmogenesis. Astronomy now regards the masses of the sun and the planets as being practically constant, so that the gravitational stresses between them are supposed to maintain a permanent configuration; it also excludes all "extra-physical" forces as having anything to do with the working of the material order. But if we at all admit the view of cosmic evolution and involution, we must hold (on *à priori* grounds at least, so long as experimental or observed facts are not forthcoming) that the stresses in the solar system (or any other system) do not maintain a *permanent* scheme of bodies; that the configuration of the planets, etc., is but approximately and relatively fixed.

The parallel of the atomic system is instructive. Here Science already recognises that the system is only relatively stable; that the electrons (unit negative charges) stepping beyond a certain "critical speed" may be dissociated from the atom and flung away; this is evidenced by radio-activity amongst other phenomena. There is nothing to prevent us from imagining that an electron moving round a central positive charge may not have an absolutely fixed orbit; that it too may either eddy towards or away from the central charge according to its adrishta; that in the former case, the electron, stepping beyond a critical rate of motion is dissociated with the result that the atom may be reconstituted (a different chemical substance may thereby be produced); and that in the latter case, the electron (negative charge) may, by curling round and round towards the central positive charge, be merged and unified with it (after a certain critical stage). This mingling of positive and negative charges means the "loss" (or dissolution) of matter—matter lapses back into Ether of which it is a strained and polarised condition. This coiling motion which we attribute to the elements of the "atom" is not unscientific, *e.g.*, the vortex-motion theory of the prime atoms is still the most promising theory of its kind.

Besides the coiling-and-uncoiling movement, the important thing to note is the "critical stage". An operation in Nature is commonly of a certain type within certain limits, but beyond them it passes into another type. There is a critical temperature (32°F) at which water become ice; another (212°F) at which it becomes steam. In all physical operations we can recognise such critical stages which mark "new" transformations or appearances or directions. In vital and psychic phenomena also we have critical stages. Increased stimulation produces increased sensation (of a certain kind) up to a limit; beyond it, it produces either no sensation or sensation of a different kind. The Mutation Theory of the Origin of Species (by Hugo De Vries) holds that new species are born out of old species suddenly like "monstrosities"; implying that the motions in the germcell overstepping a certain critical value change the character of the germ-cell itself and thus produce a new species, just under similar conditions a new atom may be evolved out of a given atom (*e.g.*, in radio-activity).

There is a further important thing to observe. In the operations of Nature, a new Principle of Control is introduced after each critical stage. When for example at 32° F water is transformed into ice, "something" appears amidst the molecules of H_2O to bring about their now shuffling or configuration; when again the germ-cell of the "anthropoid ape" "mutates" into the anthropic germcell, a new Principle of Control appears which develops it, physically and mentally, into a man rather than into an ape which is the starting datum. I need not take further illustrations, but simply note that the new Principle of Control is a new disposition of Power (Shakti) by which an old Form is transformed into a new; when, for example, by changing the "atomic number" the modern chemist hopes that he will be able to transmute a "base metal" (say mercury) into gold, he is searching after a new Principle of Control. Behind every stable special "form" in Nature there must be a special Principle of Control: a Principle of Control evolves and maintains a special rūpa and nāma in the Spiritual Ether which is in itself without rūpa and nāma. In the Veda we call each definite Principle of Control (in the sense of a Form of Chitshakti) a Devatā. Thus, all the special sense-capacities have their Devatās. The shābdic means whereby a special Principle of Control may be introduced (or invoked), is Mantra. The visual representation or optical diagram of the actual disposition of stress (Power) which constitutes a given Principle of Control, is its Yantra. And the Kriyā in general (including Mantra and Yantra) whereby a Principle of Control may be brought about or called into play, is Tantra. Kriyā here means 'functioning,' whether in the body or in the mind. When, for example, in Homa we produce fire by the mutual friction of araṇi, we are invoking a Devatā.

Recapitulating we find that in the understanding of the world-process the following points are worthy of special note:

(1) It is a finitising process—differentiating and then integrating, and then differentiating again.

(2) It is rhythmic—moving from maximum veiling to maximum manifestation and back (coiling and uncoiling).

(3) In this process there are certain critical stages at which new forms are evolved.

(4) At each critical stage there appears a new Principle of Control.

(5) A Principle of Control is the builder and sustainer of a new form.

(6) Since the world-process runs on Samaṣhti and Vyaṣhti lines, we must have a graded series (hierarchy) of critical stages and Principles of Control on both the lines.

(7) A critical stage represents a "plane" in Nature; a devatā has his adhikāra corresponding to a given plane. Suppose we take three planes in descending order—A, B. C. Then, the Principle of Control corresponding to A, has adhikāra not only over A, but also over B and C; that of B, has adhikāra (jurisdiction or competence) over B and C; that of C over C alone. Cf. the relations of Īshvara, Hiraṇya-garbha and Virāt on the Samaṣhti line.

(8) A Principle of Control on a given plane in the Samaṣhti line has control over the vyaṣhti Principle of Control on the same plane.

These properties necessarily follow from the fundamental nature of Chit. Chit is Eka, Pūrṇa and Avādhita (Svādhīna). The less it is veiled, the more will this fundamental nature express itself.

Now, veiling may involve this—the Whole is hidden and only a part displayed (finitisation); and the part displayed may be more or less obscured, *e.g.*, the jāgrat-mind of man is a vyaṣhti mind, but it is more articulate (vyakta) than his svapna-mind which in its turn is more articulate than his Suṣhupti-mind. We have this principle: the higher the plane, and the less restricted the sphere, the more patent the essential nature of Chit. Therefore, the plane being the same, a Samaṣhti Principle will have control over the Vyaṣhti Principle (because the sphere of the latter is more restricted, so that there has been greater veiling); and the extent or sphere being the same, a Principle on a higher plane will have control over a Principle on a lower plane. Thus, Vyaṣhti Prāṇa will control Vyaṣhti deha; Vyaṣhti Manas Vyaṣhti Prāṇa. There may be also, in some cases, dual control or diarchy. For instance, my mind does not seem to have complete control over the *whole* working of Prāna in my body; only *a part* of such working appears to be voluntary. In this case, the remaining part (which seems to be involuntary) is under the control of the Samaṣhti Manas (or Generic Mind), which control, may, after sādhanā, be transferred to the vyaṣhti mind in proportion as the latter assimilates itself to the Cosmic Mind by pushing back its limitations.

Without further discussing the details we may note that the critical stages or planes are broadly *five—viz.*, the five koṣhas of the Shruti (Ānandamaya, Vijnānamaya, Manomaya, Prāṇamaya and

Annamaya). They constitute a descending series of Controlling Agencies. The lower five chakras of the body as the seats of the five tattvas (kshiti, ap, tejah, marut, vyoma) illustrate this principle of higher and higher control. As we have pointed out, a higher Principle, because it is essentially Chit, will display to a greater degree the essential nature of Chit (unity, wholeness and freedom) than, a lower one. Thus, Prāṇa is more unitary, coherent and spontaneous than matter which it controls. But even matter, being essentially the same as Prāṇa, cannot by *wholly* discrete, disorganised and "determined" (inert): it is only *approximately* so. There must be a trace of unity, organisation and spontaneity (freedom) even in the material atom. The fact that the atom is a "system" is suggestive of this. Physical science works by abstraction or limitation of the data; *e.g.*, there is *really* no "rigid" body in Nature satisfying the definition of it given by Dynamics. Science deals with Fact-sections and not with the Fact. No matter-particle is therefore "dead" and *absolutely* inert.

Suppose we consider the mechanism of a matter-particle. It is like a Chinese puzzle-box—having various concentric sheaths. It *has* all the five koṣhas. But in it all except the annyamaya (gross) koṣha are yet coiled up (*i.e.*, involved, potential). One koṣha alone is uncoiled (evolved, actual), and we have motions proper to this koṣha. Physical Science deals with some of these motions (approximately), and we have the "dynamical theory" of matter. Ordinarily we have no suspicion of the 4 other koṣhas involved in the material atom. Now, suppose the motions in the outermost crust or koṣha of matter reach a certain critical stage (by reason of their adrishta or the assemblage of "subtle" stresses determining them, only *some* of which Physical Science can *approximately* compute); then, when this critical stage has been attained, the next inner koṣha (*i.e.*, Prāna) which had hitherto been coiled or involved, will "wake up" and begin to uncoil and evolve itself. The moment this happens, the so-called "dead" corpuscle will begin to appear as a living corpuscle. According to the principles explained before, a new Principle of Control, hitherto dormant (not absolutely dormant however) will appear on the scene. Its appearance will be marked by certain phenomena not clearly noticeable before—the vital phenomena. The living corpuscle will now seize upon the particles of C, H, N, O, build protoplasm, differentiate and integrate it in sundry ways, reproduce itself, and so on. In fact, by virtue of the uncoiling of the second koṣha, a new set of motions manifests itself, which was unmanifest so long as *its* plane or "scene" was folded up. So far as the play of forces is concerned, this question of "scene" is important; *e.g.*, I have stored up in me the sangskāras of 84 lacs of births (*i.e.*, kinds of birth) through which I have had passed; but in my present human life, the scene is suitable for the play of only some of those countless sangskāras and unsuitable for the play of the rest.

In a similar way, the motions in the Prāṇic koṣha, by virtue of their adriṣhta, may reach another stage at which the third or mānasic koṣha may evolve itself. Here again a new Principle of Control is introduced. In the plants the mānasic koṣha, though given, is undeveloped; so that the vital processes of the plant do not appear to be controlled by the sangkalpa of the plant itself; impulses and instincts as mental activities do not clearly appear to govern plant-life. In the animals the mind-koṣha uncoils itself; in the man and other higher beings, the Buddhi-koṣha also. They are Lower Antah-karaṇa and Higher Antah-karaṇa respectively.

It should be observed, however, that the critical stages or koṣhas are not absolute boundaries in Nature.

Like the colours in a rainbow, they give us but "working" and approximate boundaries.

Nor is it correct to regard the koṣhas as absolutely "closed curves" without mutual influence. They do, and cannot but, influence one another.

Nor again should we restrict the scope of the transformation of energy to particular koṣhas only; *i.e.*, it should not be said that the energy in the material plane and that in the Prāṇic or Mānasic plane do never transform into one another. The theory of the fundamental unity of Energy will not justify it, nor will facts warrant it. When, for example, the Chhāndogya says that the food eaten goes to build the mind, the water drunk to build the prāṇa, it is not speaking quite in a figurative sense.

The doctrine of Conservation of Energy (as an *à posteriori* generalisation) did not take into account the vast magazines of energy now discovered in the atoms; the proof of the doctrine to-day is therefore is far too difficult. We can hold the doctrine only by taking Energy *as a whole* in all its different forms (physical, prāṇic, mānasic, etc.). We hold it then as an *à priori* principle.

Suppose there is a material system consisting of the three atoms, A, B, C. Suppose also that the physical energy which they contain between them is 100. This amount excludes the vast energies which may be interned *within* the atoms themselves. 100 represents only extra-atomic energy such as heat, etc. Now, suppose by any means I am able to draw upon the energy which is contained *within* A or B or C. Since the stock is practically inexhaustible, I shall be able to do a vast deal of "work" by such intra-atomic enery; but I need not touch any part of the 100. This 100 still remains 100, though out of the given material system I am taking vast amounts of energy. Physical Science till lately knew only the 100; and stated its doctrine of transformation and conservation of energy on that basis. In fact, when we dive down to the Ether-elements themselves which compose matter, matter practically becomes dematerialised, and there material energy and vital energy may lose their "castes" or class-distinctions.

The root of the whole matter is—To what extent does a given Form release or unveil the nature of the Spiritual Ether (Chit) of which it is a mode?

We have seen that Matter as a Form of existence is more completely than any other a veiling and binding Form—though even in it we must have clear traces of unity, organisation and freedom, as Science by her discovery of atomic systems and the spontaneous "evolution" of those systems is beginning to show. What it thus restrictedly manifests is the nature of the Immense (Brahman) and the Perfect (Pūrṇa) in which everything is grounded. Life manifests or reveals the Ground more unreservedly; and it is a controlling Principle in relation to Matter inasmuch as it is a Form more expressive of the unity, wholeness and freedom of That of which it along with Matter is a Form. For the same reason also, Mind and Spirit are still superior controlling Principles. But they are all grounded in the one Immense Whole. Hence all the Forms, though distinct in their respective spheres, point to a deeper, essential unity by reason of which their operations form one common, cosmic stress-system. They can have no absolute boundaries. Not only do they condition but they transform, as regards their "matter" and "energy," into one another. They are alike in all essential respects. To take only one example: As in the atom, we have the polarity of the static and the moving charge of electricity, so in the living body, the static coiled Prāṇa-shakti at the Mūlādhāra exists (as the Tantra points out) relatively to the dynamic Prāṇa-shakti distributed over and working the bodily tissues.[1]

[1] See Arthur Avalon's "Serpent Power" where this matter is more fully explained.

To those who see the All, there is no difference except formal when Life is materialised, or when Matter is vitalised, or when Spirit is materialised, or again when everything is spiritualised.

Printed by J. R. Aria, at the Vasanta Press, Adyar, Madras.